Y0-BYA-255

5-23-13

PREVENTING DRUG ABUSE

PREVENTING DRUG ABUSE

Ideas, information, and lines of action for parents, young people, schools, and communities

A book of readings selected from current technical literature

Collected and edited by

Donald E. Barnes and Louisa Messolonghites

HOLT, RINEHART and WINSTON, Inc.
New York Toronto London Sydney

PHOTO CREDITS

XVI, 3, 4 Astor, Lenox & Tilden Foundation, New York Public Library
6 Leonard Freed
9, 10 Astor, Lenox & Tilden Foundation, New York Public Library
12, 15, 16 Medcom, Inc.
23 Arthur Tress
24 Medcom, Inc.
26 Berne Greene
32 Geoffrey Gove
36 Luis Gonzales/Erwin Kramer Photography
37 Astor, Lenox & Tilden Foundation, New York Public Library
40 Bob Combs/Rapho Guillumette, Inc.
44, 49, 50 Editorial Photocolor Archives Newsphoto
64 Michael Sterling/Editorial Photocolor Archives
67 Arthur Tress
68 Michael Hanulak/Magnum Photos, Inc.
73 Keith Hoff/Editorial Photocolor Archives
80 Berne Greene
95 Richard Bluestein
Courtesy to Horizon House, Odyssey House, and Park Slope Direction for permission to use photographs on pages 64, 36, and 95 respectively.

ACKNOWLEDGMENTS

Grateful acknowledgment is given to the following publishers, authors, and agents.

The authors and publisher have made every effort to trace the ownership of all copyrighted selections found in this book and to make full acknowledgment for their use.

ADDISON-WESLEY PUBLISHING COMPANY, INC., for "Nine Developmental Tasks of the Normal American Adolescent," by Lewis J. Judd from Medical Readings on Drug Abuse, edited by Oliver E. Byrd. Copyright © 1970 by Addison-Wesley Publishing Company, Inc. Used by permission.

AMERICAN MEDICAL ASSOCIATION for excerpt from "Youth In Rebellion: An Historical Perspective" by Stanley H. King, Ph.D., of University Health Services, Harvard University, in Drug Dependence, A Guide for Physicians. Copyright © 1969 by American Medical Association. Used by permission.

HERBERT O. BRAYER and ALLAN Y. COHEN for "Parent Approaches to Teen and Subteen Drug Abuse," by Herbert O. Brayer and Allan Y. Cohen. Copyright © 1970 by Herbert O. Brayer. Used by permission.

CALIFORNIA MEDICINE for excerpts from "Drug Abuse Recommendations for California Treatment and Research Facilities," by David E. Smith and Frederick M. Meyers in Drug Abuse Papers, 1969. Copyright © 1969 by David E. Smith and the Regents of the University of California. Used by permission.

CALIFORNIA SCHOOL HEALTH for excerpt from "The Myth of Alienation and Teen-Age Drug Use: Coming of Age In Mass Society," by Winfield W. Salisbury, Ph.D., and Frances R. Fertig, B.A., Department of Sociology, San Jose State College, San Jose, California. Used by permission.

THE CENTER FOR DRUG INFORMATION, RESEARCH AND EDUCATION, Hayward, California, and THE SCRIMSHAW PRESS, San Francisco, California, for excerpts from A New Connection: An Approach to Persons Involved in Compulsive Drug Abuse, by John H. Frykman. Copyright © 1970 by John H. Frykman. Used by permission.

COMMUNITY NEWS SERVICE, INC. for May 14, 1970 release about the drug program at James Monroe High School, Bronx, New York. Copyright © 1970 by Community News Service, Inc. Used by permission.

CROFT EDUCATIONAL SERVICES, INC. for "The Drug Problem: New Insights and Promising Approaches," by Donald E. Barnes in the November, 1970 issue of Operational Briefing, High School Principal's Service. Copyright © 1970 by Croft Educational Services, Inc. Used by permission.

1753925

COMPACT and THE EDUCATION COMMISSION OF THE STATES for excerpts from "Special Supplement: Drug Education in the States" in the December, 1970 issue of *Compact.* Copyright © 1970 by the Education Commission of the States. Used by permission.

MARCEL DEKKER, INC. for excerpts from editorial, "The Numbers Game" by Stanley Einstein from the Spring, 1968 issue of *The International Journal of the Addictions.* Copyright © 1968 by Marcel Dekker Inc. Used by permission.

for "Be Careful: More Than Drugs Are Being Sold," by Stanley Einstein from the December, 1970 issue of *The International Journal of the Addictions.* Copyright © 1970 by Marcel Dekker, Inc. Used by permission.

EDUCATION U.S.A., for "Drug Abuse Education Act of 1970," from the November 30, 1970 issue of *Education, U.S.A.* Copyright © 1970 by National School Public Relations Association. Used by permission.

ENCYCLOPEDIA BRITANNICA, INC., for *Man, Medicine and Environment* by Rene Dubos. Copyright © 1968 by Encyclopedia Britannica, Inc. Used by permission.

EMERGENCY MEDICINE MAGAZINE for excerpts from "The Trip There and Back" by David E. Smith. Copyright © 1969 by Fischer-Murray, Inc. Used by permission.

GRAFTON PUBLICATIONS, INC. for excerpts from *Addiction and Drug Abuse Reports,* May, 1970 issue. Copyright © 1970 by Grafton Publications, Inc. Used by permission.

INSTITUTE FOR DEVELOPMENT OF EDUCATIONAL ACTIVITIES, INC., I/D/E/A, an affiliate of the Charles F. Kettering Foundation, for excerpts from "An I/D/E/A Occasional Paper, High School Students and Drugs, The Report of a National Seminar, November 1969." Copyright © 1970 by the Institute for Development of Educational Activities, Inc. Used by permission.

INTERNATIONAL BUSINESS MACHINES CORPORATION: *THINK* MAGAZINE, for excerpt from "Science Assaults Another Juggernaut: *Pain*" by George A. W. Boehm in the May-June, 1970 issue of *Think* Magazine. Published by IBM. Copyright © 1970 by International Business Machines Corporation. Used by permission.

THE JOURNAL OF SCHOOL HEALTH for excerpts from "The Teen-Ager and Drug Abuse" by Frank K. Johnson and Jack Westman, in the December, 1968 issue of *The Journal of School Health.* Used by permission.

THE MACMILLAN COMPANY for excerpt from *The Loners,* short stories about the young and alienated, by L. M. Schulman. Copyright © 1970 by The Macmillan Company. Used by permission.

MANAS PUBLISHING COMPANY for excerpt from a radio commentary by Henry Anderson, station KPFA, Berkeley, California, June 17 and 18, 1966, on "The Case Against the Drug Culture," which appeared in the November 16, 1966 issue of *Manas.* Copyright © 1966 by Henry Anderson. Used by permission.

McGRAW-HILL BOOK COMPANY for excerpts from *The Drug Scene* by Donald B. Louria. Copyright © 1968 by Donald B. Louria. Used by permission.

for excerpts from *The Drug Dilemma* by Sidney Cohen. Copyright © 1969 by McGraw-Hill Book Company. Used by permission.

for excerpts from "Household Agents Pack a Deadly Punch" in the November 22, 1968 issue of *Medical World News.* Copyright © 1968 by McGraw-Hill, Inc. Used by permission.

THE MONTHLY REVIEW for excerpt from "The Political Economy of Junk" by Sol Yurick in the December, 1970 issue of *Monthly Review.* Copyright © 1970 by Sol Yurick. Used by permission.

NATIONAL ASSOCIATION OF INDEPENDENT SCHOOLS for "Drugs: Letter to a Trustee" by Edwin S. Van Gorder, III. Published in the May, 1970 issue of *The Independent School Bulletin.* Copyright © 1970 by National Association of Independent Schools. Used by permission.

NATIONAL EDUCATION ASSOCIATION for excerpts from "Suggestions for Educators" by Robert C. Petersen in the March, 1969 issue of the *NEA Journal.* Copyright © 1969 by National Education Association. Used by permission.

NEW SOCIETY for "The Marijuana Market" by Erich Goode in the June, 1970 issue of *New Society.* Copyright © 1969 by Erich Goode. Used by permission.

PANTHEON BOOKS, a division of RANDOM HOUSE, INC., for excerpts from *Mainline to Nowhere: The Making of a Heroin Addict* by Yves J. Kron and Edward M. Brown. Copyright © 1965 by Yves. J. Kron and Edward M. Brown. Used by permission.

for excerpt from *The New Handbook of Prescription Drugs* by Richard Burack. Copyright © 1970 by Richard Burack. Used by permission.

GEORGE A. PFLAUM PUBLISHERS for "Revolution for the Sell of It" by Sal Giarrizzo from *See* Magazine, published September, 1970. Copyright © 1970 by Screen Educators Society, Inc. Used by permission.

POCKET BOOKS, a division of SIMON & SCHUSTER, INC., for excerpt from *Nightmare Drugs* by Donald B. Louria. Copyright © 1966 by Mel Sokolow Associates. Used by permission.

RAND McNALLY AND CO., for excerpts from "Cultural Differences in Rates of Alcoholism" by Robert Freed Bales in *Deviate Behavior and Social Process,* edited by William A. Rushing. Copyright © 1969 by Rand McNally & Co. Used by permission.

RANDOM HOUSE, INC. for excerpt from *Crisis in the Classroom* by Charles E. Silberman. Copyright © 1970 by Charles E. Silberman. Used by permission.

TRANS-ACTION for "The Health of Haight-Ashbury" by David E. Smith, John Luce and Ernest A. Dernberg in the April, 1970 issue of *Trans*-action. Copyright © 1970 by *Trans*-action, Inc., New Brunswick, New Jersey. Used by permission.

SCHOLASTIC VOICE for "Guidelines for Working with Students," by Jerry Levine. Copyright © 1971 by Scholastic Magazines. Used by permission.

VAN NOSTRAND REINHOLD for excerpt from *Toward A Psychology of Being,* Second Edition, by Abraham H. Maslow. Copyright © 1968 by Litton Educational Publishing, Inc. Used by permission.

WYETH LABORATORIES for excerpts from *The Sinister Garden.* Copyright © 1966 by Wyeth Laboratories. Used by permission.

DEDICATED

TO

THE BROTHERHOOD ESTABLISHMENT

FOREWORD

The acute interest of the Institute for Educational Development (IED) in prevention of drug abuse began with a search for model drug education programs in response to requests of two major high schools in New York City, James A. Monroe (Bronx) and Louis D. Brandeis (Manhattan). That undertaking was made possible by the sponsorship of the Economic Development Council of New York City, acting in the interests of better education.

Over a period of 18 months or so we have created a document which may be useful to parents, teachers and young people concerned about drugs. We ourselves are "parents, teachers and young people." We are not drug experts. We are deeply concerned. In the process of developing this anthology, IED's staff surveyed the bulk of recent professional literature related to drug education, and examined a considerable portion of the recent literature in pharmacology, etiology of drug dependency, demographic studies of addiction, descriptions of current treatment and rehabilitation programs, and a broad spectrum of contemporary culture and sub-culture critics and interpreters whose works touch upon drugs.

Our primary interest was, and is, prevention, not treatment. It seemed justifiable to suppose that somewhere—and perhaps in numerous places—people might be making progress with preventive programs. Current efforts at discouraging drug experimenters might have better chances for success than attempts to cure addicts. So we searched the country for programs aimed at prevention, and were forced to acknowledge the low state of preventive programs in schools as of 1971.

Our staff talked with scores of top people committed professionally and personally to the battle against drug abuse, and though we found some programs that seemed to be pointed in productive directions, we were unable to find a model for inner-city high schools where the drug problem was heroin, not marijuana. We were tacitly advised by specialists that if we wanted a model to exist, we might have to invent one. But that is another story, some of which is reported in chapter six of this volume.

In the meantime, IED also served as consulting staff to the New York State Education Department in preparing guidelines for schools on prevention of drug abuse, and performed other functions for a Task Force on Drug Education assembled by that department.

IED's work in drug education has been headed by Donald E. Barnes, with notable assistance from Louisa Messolonghites. Associates who have aided them include

Bernard Mackler, Aida Price, Lea Guyer, and Shirley Robinson.

We are grateful to hundreds of persons who have taken time to assist us in large and small ways, and we single out some individuals for special mention who gave us their scarcest commodity—time: David E. Smith, M.D., and the staff of the Haight-Ashbury Clinic, San Francisco; Herbert O. Brayer and Zella W. Cleary, Coronado (California) Unified School District; Lura Jackson, National Institute of Mental Health; Stanley Einstein, Institute for the Study of Drug Addiction; Gerald Edwards, Department of Health Education, Adelphi University; Stephen Gross, Assistant Dean, Columbia University College of Pharmaceutical Sciences, Roswell D. Johnson, M.D., Director of Health Services, Brown University; former Commissioner Martin Kotler, New York City Addiction Services Agency; Oliver E. Byrd, M.D., Department of Health Education, Stanford University; Assistant Commissioner Robert Dolins, and Robert A. Fox, New York State Narcotics Addiction Control Commission; John S. Sinacore and Leo W. Denault, New York State Education Department Special Unit on Drug Education; Sherman W. Patrick and William Edwards, Narcotics Institute Preventive Program; Beny Prim, M.D., Narcotic Addiction and Treatment Corporation; Richard Brotman, Director of the Division of Community Health, New York Medical College; Patricia Hill, California State Board of Education; John J. Cohrssen, Senior Staff Associate, President's Advisory Council on Executive Organization; Jay Cutler, Special Assistant to Senator Jacob Javits; special agents of the Bureau of Narcotics and Dangerous Drugs, Department of Justice (who requested anonymity); and the Superintendent of Documents (who deserves a final tribute).

Then we must mention some of those who have contributed to this volume and to our understanding by sharing their common problems and concerns, methods and high motivations, mistakes and mystiques: Jerry Levine, Drug Information Services Director, James H. Monroe High School, and the membership of the Brotherhood Establishment (about which, more will be said); Alex Weinstein, Narcotics Coordinator, Louis D. Brandeis High School; Pat Spellman and Charles Franklin, Phoenix House Encounter group leaders; Robert Young, East Harlem Youth Employment Service; and Sharon Hewlett, Manpower Career Development Agency. Wai Fun Chin and Jade Chang, students and later graduates of the New York City Central Commercial High School, shared responsibilities in acquiring, indexing, filing and retrieving documents, and in offering polite and wise advice on ways to save time and paper.

Sidney P. Marland, Jr.
Formerly, President,
Institute for Educational Development

CONTENTS

PREFACE

The concern over drug use in this country symbolizes one of the paradoxes of the times in which certain technical advances leapfrog over our moral means for coping with them. "Drug education" carries the connotation of "stop it" to both adults and students. Until recently, the speakers most commonly invited to address local groups of P.T.A., church, service clubs, etc., were enforcement officials rather than sociologists, psychologists or physicians. It is reassuring for parents to hear about "stricter enforcement" as the most effective solution, despite the fact that few knowledgeable professionals outside the enforcement field find this answer convincing.

Every knowledgeable professional faces a hazardous choice in addressing young people. If he adopts a "hard" traditional line on all drugs, he risks losing his audience; if he does not choose the "hard" line on everything, including marijuana, he risks losing his job. A speaker may unwittingly be counter-productive even with the best of intentions when, for instance, his disapproval of the unnecessarily harsh marijuana laws is construed by students (as well as some adults) as an advocacy of *no* controls, which is decidedly different. Occasionally attempts to be explicit ricochet. A typical Sunday supplement feature on the multi-faceted drug problem will, for instance, run illustrative photographs or diagrams for needle use. Commenting in a Letter to the Editor, an ex-addict now doing rehabilitation work congratulated one such newspaper for having printed the best primer that he had seen on how to use heroin.

We must keep reminding ourselves that young people using drugs are somebody's children. Both in the public domain and private experience, we know that the use of marijuana is so highly pervasive that no segment of society has escaped it. If parents are powerless to prevent involvement of their children, it is fatuous to shift that responsibility to enforcement officials. "Pusher" is virtually an obsolete word. He doesn't have to "push." We don't term the package store owner a "pusher;" he is known as a dealer. Similarly, the prototype distributor of drugs today is a "dealer." Almost always the dealer is indistinguishable from anyone else in the buyer's peer group; he is not the slinking character in a dark trench coat with his hat down over his eyes. He, likewise, is somebody's child.

Most college students accept a distinction between the user and abuser of drugs. In their culture, heroin is not an accepted drug. Amphetamines are generally acceptable only in the oral form used to combat fatigue.

Use or abuse of marijuana is judged chiefly by the frequency with which it is used. Even with LSD, frequency of usage has become the measure of the abuser. We adults have long been accustomed to classifying our drinking companions by their intake during a given period, and their discernible reactions to the quantity consumed. There is a significant segment of society that considers any internal use of alcohol an abuse. Young people use similar gradations in placing the borderlines between users and abusers.

The lecture approach to drug education has but limited value. It is best suited to adults seeking knowledge about pharmacology, physical and psychological reactions to the various substances, symptoms and manifestations to alert them to danger signals. The primary purpose of the lecture is to impart knowledge to a highly motivated group; any alteration of behavior resulting from the knowledge is a desirable side-effect that should not be anticipated. The lecture may also have some value to nonusing students as reinforcement of their tentative decision to stay away from drugs. Here again, we are not trying to alter behavior. For a speaker, however, this setting may well be the most delicate. He must be certain that any statement that he makes has substantial backing in pertinent, authoritative data; if it is an opinion, it must be one of tempered judgment, without clear alignment of polarity.

Balance must be maintained by mentioning certain generally accepted attitudes toward drugs which are not altogether adverse. To do otherwise may put the young auditor in an untenable position when he chooses to defend his thesis against arguments and temptations from drug-oriented peers. As Robert Louis Stevenson said, "The truth that is suppressed by friends is the readiest weapon of the enemy."

Certainly the public is vitally interested in "sure and final" data on all drugs. Dr. Chauncey Leake, Professor of Pharmacology at the University of California states, "Let us remember that whatever truth we may get by scientific study about ourselves and our environment is always relative, tentative, subject to change and corrections, and there are not final answers."

Those who would discourage experimentation (even with drugs) in the bright, inquisitive young people of today have a most difficult assignment. There is so little left to explore without a NASA-sized budget that new experience is sought in high-risk outlets such as sky-diving, scuba-diving, motor-biking and drug use. The first three activities are admittedly dangerous and deaths are not unusual, yet only to drug taking does society assign a moral stigma and seek to imprison the participant.

There is no consensus on the format to discourage drug experimentation and usage. Leaders in the field of psychology, anthropology, education, medicine and law enforcement are attempting to influence behavior through their own orientations, either singly or collectively. It becomes more and more obvious that no single discipline can solve the problem. It remains to be seen what can be accomplished with a collective effort. A broad-based rational approach without undue polarity is needed. From a wide sampling of the experience of various workers in the drug field, this collection of data and discussions has been assembled. It represents the best efforts to date in the achievement of the rational approach.

Roswell D. Johnson, M. D.
Director of Health Services
Brown University

INTRODUCTION

What are the grounds for hope in trying to prevent drug abuse? What approaches seem to be making headway? What clues have the professionals and laymen found for helping people withdraw from experimental use of mind-bending and body-damaging chemical substances? What are the chances of retrieving those who are in the advanced stages of drug abuse? What motivates their behavior? Where are the most promising school programs? What can parents, families, teachers, guidance counsellors, students, social workers, police, nurses, and other professional and concerned persons do? What answers are offered to questions, and what new questions are being asked?

Our purpose in presenting these readings is to respond to these questions insofar as satisfactory replies could be found in published sources, primarily in articles written for specialized audiences. Many of the ideas and research results in the technical literature have not appeared in popular publications and are unavailable, in a practical sense, to both lay and professional persons, as well as to organizations and institutions, short of a large-scale effort such as ours.

What are the tidings for the future? The weight of opinion seems to be affirmative in the many hundreds of articles and books we have searched. As the reader will see, the balance of the evidence is toward guarded optimism, toward indications that we can expect better understanding of behavior related to drugs with increased knowledge and fuller, fairer discussion of the subject. Feasible and increasingly efficient methods of prevention are developing, and the upsurge of drug abuse experienced in the U.S. during the 1960's probably can be contained and perhaps even decreased.

Those are conjectural conclusions, of course. We could encounter new and worse situations. The laboratories could produce perilous and unimagined drugs by the score and many new cults and sorcerers could appear among us. Arthur Koestler predicts that in ten years tranquilizers will be replaced by "harmonizers", chemicals that will integrate the functions of the "old" brain (dominated by emotions) with the "new" (neo-cortex, concerned with reason, symbolic thought, abstractions) thus "stabilizing people, . . . harmonizing them without really castrating them, without sterilizing them mentally." (*The New York Times Magazine*, August 30, 1970, p. 24.)

Some experts fear that people may continue to turn from each other and toward drugs, *en masse*. Stanley Einstein, a prominent psychologist, in his article, "Drug Use and Misuse in the 1970's," warns, "Taking drugs is the danger sign of the fact that most of the population turns to things rather than to people for their everyday legitimate needs. . . . The 1970's should be a decade not of "drug" research, but of investigating ways for people to live with themselves and each other, given the combination of the old and new pressures that we will experience. Research must be tied into preventive measures which not only focus upon stopping something, but give us alternatives for starting— for building something; and that something should be not only for a person but for his community as well."

Nevertheless a cautiously favorable prognosis seems to be justified by recent indications that a community, or school, or even a family or individual can take effective preventive measures.

The term "prevention" has different meanings to people working in the fields associated with drug abuse. It may be used in the sense of "preventive maintenance," of helping someone before a more serious breakdown occurs. Prevention also means assisting persons in stages of drug abuse short of psychological or physical dependence. It is also used in the epidemiological sense. Generally the term applies to educational as distinct from medical efforts.

The line is often blurred between preventive programs and the treatment and rehabilitation of addicts. A useful classification for preventive programs might be borrowed from the system used for assigning priorities for wounded patients arriving at military field hospitals. After screening, patients were assigned to one of three groups: Those who would probably recover without immediate treatment; those whose chances of recovery seemed to depend upon immediate treatment; and those considered hopeless. Care, of course, was given first to patients in the second group and at certain times *only* to that group.

For obvious reasons the public outcry and private fears have focused on opiate addiction. Most of the research and development programs have sought knowledge and techniques concerned with the causes and treatment of opiate addiction. Public health authorities have placed a high priority on rehabilitation of addicts, and public funds have been allocated accordingly.

It is not our purpose here to dispute the wisdom of these policies, nor to question the efficacy of methods now used for treatment and rehabilitation of addicts nor even to present information on those subjects. The activities of investigators and program developers working with addicts, and some of the difficulties they face, seem to be poorly understood by an impatient public. Perhaps our engineering coups—transmission of signals, cybernetics, moonshots—make us forgetful that, despite consensus among taxpayers supporting research appropriations, many of man's problems, including narcotics addiction, simply will not yield to solution according to PERT schedules.

We are also omitting arguments from the debate on legalization or liberalization of marijuana laws, a subject that shows little evidence of neglect in the media and minds of a public re-examining its motives and morals.

One of the vexations for those trying to prevent drug abuse lies in the extreme difficulty they encounter in proving that they are achieving what they set out to do. Because of unreported events, unreliability of informants, and partisanship in the handling and reporting of data, startling disparities often appear in statistics announced by governmental officials, even within the same agency.

As an illustration of the difficulties that go with nose-counting and drugs, an August 23, 1970 edition of *The New York Times Magazine* reports that the National Institute of Mental Health estimated in October, 1969 that about 5 million juveniles and adults had used marijuana at least once. Five months later, another NIMH pamphlet said that "more than 8 million people have used the drug." Only a month later the NIMH reported to Congress that the number "conservatively was between 8 million and 12 million." Sixty days thereafter, according to *The Times*, figure was put at 20 million.

Trustworthy evidence, therefore, as to what kinds of people in the community or school are using how much of what kinds of drugs seldom can be obtained. Once in hand, such evidence may become obsolete very quickly and may have value mainly as information against which later studies might try to measure changes.

The history of the drug phenomenon in the United States in the 1960's remains to be written, and the job will be made difficult by the scarcity of credible statistics on people drugging themselves.

As preceding paragraphs suggest, hard data that will demonstrate reduction of drug abuse as a direct result of prevention programs probably are not to be found at this time. Nonetheless, we have included interesting and persuasive readings which describe community programs that the program developers and participants believe are acting as successful deterrents, both in the epidemiological sense and in help brought to young persons in the process of turning off drugs.

In searching the literature, we noted that information on drugs themselves was quite readily available in both popular and technical sources. Therefore, early in the process of selecting readings for this volume, we decided to make room for less accessible material and to deal only incidentally, if at all, with pharmacology, toxicology, and the pseudochemistry of the drug culture. (Most of the readings included in this anthology are brief excerpts from full texts which are available. Sources appear either before or after each excerpt.)

Perhaps that decision was influenced by the fact that we felt better qualified for scholarly tasks in the social sciences than in biology. The main reason, however, grew from our doubts concerning the value of imparting technical information on drugs as a means of preventing drug abuse. For a long time that practice has been the central theme of nearly all prevention programs. And what group of people have been better *informed* as to the nature and effects of drugs, including potential dangers, than physicians? Yet, we know from various sources that, compared with other occupational groups, physicians have shown high susceptibility to narcotics addiction and drug abuse.

We have observed, along with others, that student drug discussion groups soon leave the pharmacological aspects of the subject and move into questions which seem to them more vital. With deep and persistent interest they ask each other: What is fair? What is the best kind of life? How can I decide what is right and whether something

is true? Whom should I trust? They seem to associate such questions with their decisions about using drugs.

We noted the same difficulty on the part of groups of teachers or addicts. The substances which people administer to themselves, however morbid and potentially harmful, appear to be much less absorbing and relevant subjects for discussion than the dilemmas, decision processes, and motivations of the users. Drugs are not wrong or evil or injurious in their own nature. They do not insinuate themselves into human bodies. They are things *which people administer to themselves.*

This line of thought, urged in recent years by Levy, Cohen, Einstein, and other leading students of the drug scene, provides one of the key assumptions for preventive programs in the 1970's. As Marvin R. Levy has stated, "Drugs *per se* are not the issue; rather the issue is why people use them."

The concern of this book, then, is for people, and its scope is limited to ways of understanding and influencing certain human behavior. We are interested in increasing the alternatives individuals have for making decisions as to how to live well, and with lasting satisfaction. However else an addict may be described, he is the penultimate example of someone who possesses very few options. And whatever chemicals may offer in temporary respite from pain, tension, fatigue, boredom, or anxiety, they have been shown to diminish the capacities of human beings to perceive and to exercise control over their environment. Some of the chemicals, of course, can be physically destructive, as in the case of reported direct and indirect effects on the brain and liver associated with the use of alcohol. And if it is consumed in excess, any substance appears to be unhealthy or even poisonous to the human body.

These general observations on drugs have been offered to reveal the editors' assumptions and biases in the preparation of what is essentially a people-oriented book. The enormity of the job of preventing drug abuse may be more clearly seen if it is described as helping people understand and depend upon each other, and upon themselves, rather than upon chemicals.

Chapter One

PERSPECTIVES AND DIRECTIONS

Man's need for drugs seems rooted in his persistent belief in the marvelous powers of little-understood substances introduced into the human body. To be understood at all, our drug culture must be seen in its ancient as well as its modern context. Our frame of reference includes the monk's philtre which transported Juliet, the pot-liquor brewed by Shakespear's witches, and also, the dried bugs prescribed by South Seas' witchdoctors. The Greeks anticipated the experience of subsequent eras including our own and used both their religion and practical arts, medical practice especially, to develop basic attitudes toward the use of drugs.

If anyone chooses to read this book instead of a hundred other books dealing with the drug problem, his decision may indicate faith in the ability of man to work his way out of problems that seem, in certain contexts, insoluble.

We do not believe that this or any book, or any drug prevention program, will prevent the use of drugs to the extent of making everybody abstinent. People, apparently, are unwilling or unable to put up with their own behavior, much less the next man's, without resorting to chemicals.

Distinction Between Prevention and Treatment

Those who search for meanings in the current drug culture would do well to consult the writings of Rene Dubos, microbiologist, experimental pathologist, and author of *The Torch of Life*, *The Unseen World*, *The Dreams of Reason*, *The White Plague*, *The Mirage of Health*, *Man Adapting*, and *So Human an Animal*. Dubos makes a distinction that should be kept in mind in addressing the subject of drugs—the distinction between prevention and treatment.

Two goddessess, Hygieia (Health) and Panacea (All Heal or Cure All) represented the medical practices in Greek mythology. Hygieia was one of the manifestations of Athena, the goddess of reason. She was concerned not so much with the treatment of disease as with its prevention and with the maintenance of health. She symbolized the belief that men would remain healthy if they lived wisely, within the golden rule, and according to the laws of reason. *Mens sana in corpore sano* remains today the goal of all-embracing hygiene, even though men have found it difficult to do more than pay lip service to the teachings of Hygieia.

Panacea specialized in the knowledge of drugs. She symbolized the belief that ailments can be cured by skillful use of the proper kinds of substances derived either from plants or from the earth. The illusion that drugs can solve all medical problems survives today in our use of the word "panacea."

Hygieia and Panacea . . . were specifically mentioned in the opening invocation of the Hippocratic Oath . . . ancient physicians differentiated between prevention and treatment of disease and recognized the importance of both types of medical activity. Greek legend thus anticipated some of the most important theoretical attitudes of modern medicine.

Rene Dubos in *Man, Medicine, and Environment*.

Historical Perspective

To understand a culture one must know the myths and history that have shaped that culture. Rebellion has a place in American myth and history, and our next selection focuses on the sometimes constructive results of rebellion.

The active rebelliousness of youth which seems so characteristic of this day and age is not unique. In ancient history an observer of the Egyptian scene recorded: "Our earth is degenerate . . . children no longer obey their parents." We know that Socrates expressed concern about the young men of Athens: their long hair, their indolence, and their disdain for adult values. In more recent history there are some interesting accounts about students at Harvard College.

In 1776, [students at Harvard] broke out a rebellion which raged for a month. Two years later "great disturbances" occurred; the tutors windows were broken with brickbats, their lives endangered, and other outrages committed.

The next important rebellions occurred in 1807, when the three lower classes protested against the bad food at Commons. Without waiting for the president to investigate and correct, they indulged in disorders. . . . The troubles increased, and with them the alarm of the faculty. . . . A few days later

the four classes marched out in a body from dinner, complaining of the fare. . . . The corporation met, and ordered the president to attend Commons "on Sunday morning next," adding that "in consideration of the youth of the students, and hoping that their rash and illegal conduct is rather owing to want of experience and reflection than to malignity of temper or a spirit of defiance, (the corporation) are disposed to give them an opportunity to certify in writing to the president, as he shall direct, their admission of the impropriety of their conduct, their regret for it, and their determination to offend no more in this manner." Seven days were allowed for this confession to be made, but, although the time was extended, some of the students refused. . . .

If we but alter the style of writing a bit, the words have a familiar ring. Rebellion by the young is not new. . . .

. . . the transition through adolescence is more likely to be a time of crisis, upheaval, and rebellion under different social conditions. Prominent among these is social change. This occurs when there are significant shifts in political power, in the economic structure of the society, when there are important alterations in the value system, and when the social expectations for behavior in adult roles become fuzzy or confused.

The particular content of a value system, that is, the kinds of things that are emphasized, is also important. When the individual is regarded as more important, more worthwhile than the social group, there is more likelihood of crisis in adolescence. Social and personal upheaval is more apt to ensue if dissent is part of the cultural heritage, if man is regarded as able to control and alter nature rather than be subject to it, and if change and progress are considered a goal to be achieved rather than a drawback to be avoided.

When these social conditions are present, the likelihood of crisis and rebellion during adolescence is enhanced. . . .

Crisis, however, does not always lead to rebellion. We need only to refer to our knowledge of defense and coping mechanisms to spell out the potential consequences. One reaction can be regression and disintegration. This is likely to occur in psychologically vulnerable individuals when social disruption is severe. We noticed it in the United States when the plains Indian tribes were driven onto reservations and prevented from following the whole fabric of life they had known in the past.

Passive withdrawal also occurs, a condition more akin to the old phrase, "out of sight, out of mind." Here there is a resignation, a lack of effort, almost a waiting until the storm passes, a withdrawing in upon the self as if to still the feeling of anxiety and crisis.

Rebellion is one form of active engagement with the environment and involves a mobilization of aggressive energy for outward thrust. It can easily become destructive and erupt in a blind tearing of the fabric of social order. Rage becomes the dominant theme, untempered by reason, unguided by a sense of love and concern for others. Destructive rebellion is like the severe temper tantrums of childhood.

Rebellion can also have a coping rather than a defensive quality and be constructive. Throughout the ages man has changed his environment in order to find new solutions for perceived deficiencies in the past. Though to the adult world this kind of rebellion may have radical aspects, it often contains the elements of a more viable and stronger social structure.

Few would deny that significant changes are taking place in the social structure and general fabric of life today in the United States and in other countries. These changes are based, at least in part, on technological advances which have come with ever increasing rapidity. . . .

We can lose perspective easily and feel that all adolescents are moving toward personal disintegration, withdrawal, or destructive rage. It is easy to forget that the majority may be taking a more constructive path, even though it appears to us as rebellion. We may not like their dress, or customs, or manner of rebelling, or their questioning our values. The sense of security in our adult position may be threatened. Perhaps, however, a significant number of the younger generation feel a sense of urgency about the world which we do not understand fully and a conviction that social change must occur more rapidly than at any time in the past, if mankind is to survive. They could be right! They will not find the answer in drugs, for they will, in the long run, be too busy throwing their energies into confronting the world with new solutions to social and political crises we have not foreseen.

Dr. Stanley H. King, Ph.D., as Director of Research, Harvard University Health Services, Harvard University, in his article "Youth In Rebellion: An Historical Perspective," in *Drug Dependence: A Guide for Physicians*.

Jackson experimenting on himself with the reaction to ether.

It comes as a surprise to many people to learn that children are getting high on airplane glue and other inhalants. But there are also historical antecedents for sniffing. Dr. Sidney Cohen recalls earlier carefree times when various fumes were inhaled for fun. We follow his account with a recent anecdote that shows, among other things, that young people do pick up *some* ideas from history.

The historical antecedents of our present-day sniffers were the venerable anesthetic inhalers. It is remarkable that all three of the original general anesthetics—ether, chloroform, and nitrous oxide —were used as intoxicating agents even before they were known to be anesthetics. During the nineteenth century, chloroform parties were held at Cambridge University and elsewhere until its toxicity became evident. The safer ether was more widespread as a source of fun. For a while in Ireland ether threatened to displace alcohol. Ether frolics were well known: "The students at Harvard used to inhale sulfuric ether from their handkerchiefs, and it intoxicated them and made them reel and stagger." W. T. G. Morton, "A Memoir to the Academy of Sciences at Paris on a New Use of Sulphuric Ether," *Littel's Living Age*, 529–571 (March 18), 1848.

Even more widespread was the use of laughing gas, or nitrous oxide. College students, writers, high society, and those who were willing to spend a quarter at county-fair laughing gas exhibitions all discovered the delightful and hilarious inebriation. This mundane anesthetic, now administered for dental extractions and minor surgery, is of interest to us for historical and current reasons. First, it was the primary nineteenth-century psychedelic. Some of the descriptions of its effects rival those of today's reports of chemical psychedelic encounters. William James, whose *Varieties of Religious Experience* remains a classic, considered nitrous oxide to be a mind-expanding substance. Consider the following anonymous report:

> I have reached infinity. I have been able to dissociate myself from this world. Life on earth becomes a fleeting split-second memory in the realm of the universe. During one session I was conscious of the fact that if I really wanted to find the answers to life, I would have to die. And I am convinced that I could have died if I wanted to pursue my search further. My body would eventually be suspended, completely dissociated from this world in a Godlike state. Under withdrawal of the substance, atoms, sound, and light rapidly fell back into place like a jigsaw puzzle, revealing to my great astonishment and disappointment the reality of this life and this world, which had just been no more than a tiny segment, a remote memory on this greater world of which I was privileged to be a part. These experiences were actually religious in spite of the fact that I am not religious at all.

This is an extract of some notes taken after a dental procedure employing laughing gas.

Currently an occasional young person is found to be a laughing-gas inhaler. Cylinders and aerosols of the gas are available from hospital-supply dealers and even more widely from industry. It is used as a whipped-cream propellant, for the ignition of racing cars, and in other industrial processes. It is therefore widely and easily available. In the coming years more people may rediscover this agent.

Sidney Cohen, M. D., in *The Drug Dilemma*.

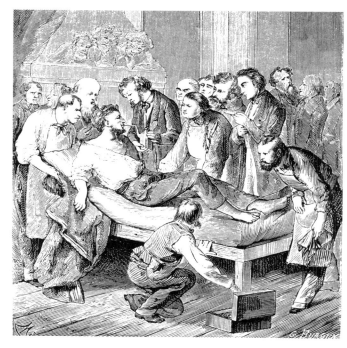

Morton making the first use of ether for a surgical operation in a Boston hospital.

A wave of thefts of ether by young people was observed by government drug officials [during the] summer [of 1969]. "Kids were swiping ether all over the country," was the word. . . . Only possible explanation was that, two weeks earlier, the National Institute of Mental Health had reprinted a classic article, "Ether Drinking" by Norman Kerr, which had first been published in 1890. Drinking of ether was a not uncommon form of drug abuse in the latter part of the last century; the substance produced quick intoxication, which rapidly passed away, leaving no hangover; this made ether popular before its toxic qualities were understood. . . . The reprint had not been circulated among the young, but had apparently hit the drug culture within a fortnight anyway . . .

Addiction and Drug Abuse Report of May, 1970.

Behavior Modification Drugs

Dr. Theodore Gordon of the Institute for the Future foresaw in 1969 that "perhaps tomorrow we will have the pharmaceutical equivalent of the liquor store in which chemicals can be obtained to buy any mood, from euphoria to mystic contemplation. Wives, perhaps, will slip anti-grouch pills into their husband's morning coffee." And the husband, if he reads the pharmaceutical news, might retaliate with a dash of *oxanamide* in her morning tea. (This is a relatively new concoction to "improve the behavior of the 'chronically irritated' female patient," according to Robert S. DeRopp in his revised edition of *Drugs and the Mind*.)

"It may become necessary to establish new legal and moral codes to govern those who prescribe use of psychedelic drugs," warned Dr. Glenn T. Seaborg, former chairman of the United States Atomic Energy Commission, in 1962. He was concerned especially that drugs such as LSD might be prescribed for a person in a position of authority who is faced with making decisions of great consequence. Though he was speculating before a graduating class about a future thirty years hence, in which pharmaceuticals could be used to change and maintain human personality at any desired level, less than a decade had passed when the students read in the daily press testimony bearing out Dr. Seaborg's concern.

John Holt, teacher and author, spoke before a Congressional committee investigating the use of amphetamines on elementary school children. He cited misgivings about the use of behavior-modification drugs to treat learning disabilities in school children: "Children have a great deal of energy; they like to move about; they live and learn with their bodies and muscles, not just their eyes and ears; when adults try to compel them to remain still and silent for long periods of time they resent and resist it; most of them can be cowed and silenced by various bribes and threats; five to 15 percent cannot. These we diagnose as suffering from a "learning malady called *hyperkinesis*".

Hyperkinesis is also called the problem-child syndrome. As chairman of the Right to Privacy Inquiry, Congressman Cornelius Gallagher (D.N.J.) stated that "there is a very great temptation to diagnose the bored but bright child as hyperactive, prescribe drugs, and thus deny him full learning during his most creative years."

Dr. Thomas C. Points, a Deputy Assistant Secretary of the Department of Health, Education and Welfare, testified before the same committee and cited 38 studies over the years that show evidence that children suffering from hyperkinesis, or minimal brain dysfunction, have been helped by prescriptions of certain stimulant drugs, including amphetamines. Dr. Points further called attention to state laws that require parental consent before children could be treated with drugs.

The committee also heard from Mrs. Daniel Youngs. A school principal read the report card of Mrs. Youngs' daughter and made an "astonishing diagnosis." Though he had never seen her daughter, the principal informed Mrs. Youngs, "Your daughter has minimal brain dysfunction." Mrs. Youngs complained that for the next few years she was constantly harassed for refusing permission to have her daughter treated with drugs.

Two psychiatrists who have used drugs since 1955 to treat hyperactivity and resulting disorders of learning have stated that the typical response to the drug is a decrease in unfocused and unproductive activity; and that there is an increase in ability to concentrate to the degree that the child is able to achieve at a higher level in school, is less impulsive and disruptive in the classroom and on the playground, and is better accepted by his peers. The doctors, John E. Peters and Sam D. Clements of the University of Arkansas Medical Center, recommended the judicious use of medications as part of a total treatment program to prevent the development of negative personal and social consequences later in life.

The Congressional investigation was triggered by a story in the *Washington Post* about an estimated 3,000 to 6,000 children in Omaha, Nebraska, public schools, who were given amphetamines, a drug classified by the government as a "dangerous substance." The shockwaves were still reverberating in the press, as of October 13, 1970, when plans were announced by the Nixon Administration to convene a scientific panel to warn doctors and educators about the possible effects of the abuse of "behavior modification" drugs to calm overactive school children. Announcing the plan, Edward F. Ziegler, Director of the Office of Child Development, told listeners to the "Washington Window" radio program, "I am very much afraid that many teachers in this nation are utilizing this as a way out of the difficulties of the classrooms."

Meanwhile, Dr. Frank H. Ayd, Jr., psychiatrist and editor of the *International Drug Therapy Newsletter*, explained to the American Chemical Society that there would be less abuse of drugs if more effective drugs for treatment were legalized, and complained that the United States is two to seven years behind European countries in approving the use of certain drugs for treatment—"I suppose it's the arch-conservative attitude of the Federal Drug Administration."

Dr. Ayd told the scientists, "We used to think of depression as an illness of people in their 30's and 40's, but now we find it widespread among young people, even children. Youngsters who try "medicating themselves" out of depression often end up with a need for the wrong drug which is damaging their health. We need more effective anti-depressants which work quicker and have less side effects that interfere with performance."

The public will continue to debate how to use the new knowledge that is being acquired about biochemistry and personality.

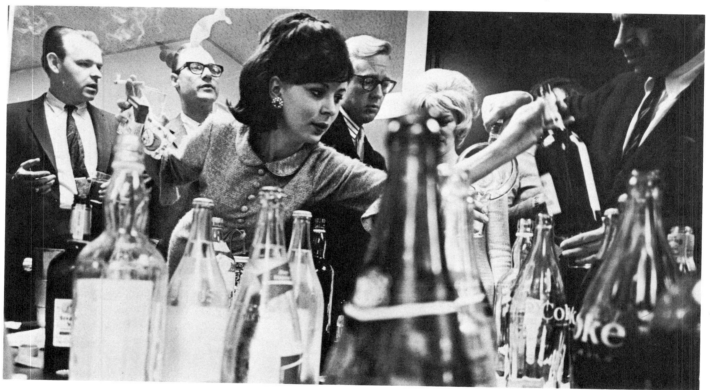

Defining the "User" and the "Abuser"

Through lack of definition of terms, misunderstanding on the subject of drugs abounds. For our own purposes, administration of a prescription drug without a prescription generally amounts to abuse, and in such cases the "user" is said to be "abusing." Who will disagree that anything more than moderate consumption of alcohol amounts to abuse? Thus, for the purpose of definition a very substantial segment of the adult American population qualifies for the label *drug user*. According to Earl Ubell, CBS science editor, perhaps four million persons are *addicted* to alcohol in the sense that "they cannot give it up either psychologically or physically." Thus, he points out, "one drug causes more human trouble than all others combined."

Senator Harold E. Hughes, Chairman of the Senate Special Subcommittee on Alcoholism and Narcotics, stated his conviction in 1969 that more than 12 million Americans are alcoholics.

The large-scale consumption of amphetamines by women for presumed appetite reduction suggests that drug abuse is by no means primarily masculine behavior. Nor is it confined to a single age group. Grownups, perhaps not surprisingly, seem to understand their own kind of drug abuse more readily than those who are not yet adults, hence the definitions of younger "users" which follow may be helpful.

. . . we should clarify the terms drug use and drug user. Much of the confusion that exists in the reporting and interpreting of statistics and in journalistic generalizations has arisen because of lack of definition of these terms. A large number of the so-called drug users have merely used drugs on one or a few occasions. In contrast to these there does exist a group for which I would prefer to reserve the term user. Students make a clear distinction between those who briefly experiment with a drug and those for whom use of the drug has at least temporarily become an important factor in their lives. The latter they call "heads". . . . The danger in not distinguishing between the casual experimenter and the "head" is that it can lead us to erroneous generalizations and assumptions both about the students and the drugs. . . .

Helen Nowlis, Professor of Psychology, University of Rochester, in "Communicating About Drugs," a speech made at the National Association of Student Personnel Administrations Drug Conference, Washington, D.C., Nov. 1966, published in the *NIMH Resource Book for Drug Abuse Education.*

Categorizing Drug Users

There are many ways of categorizing drug users, and it would be helpful to have a common terminology for the various stages a person may enter along the continuum of use. How many times must a person experiment before he becomes a periodic user? a regular user? a "head"?

Dr. David E. Smith makes his distinctions in motivational terms:

The experimental user is the beginner. In our research, we've found that the primary motivation in the early teens is curiosity and group conformity. These kids want to know what "being high" is. Their friends are using drugs, so they decide that they want to try them. The trouble is that the experimental user is very often unsophisticated about what a high is. He'll try anything he's heard will give him one, and sometimes it isn't even a real high, it's just a toxic reaction.

They begin young. We've seen one patient at the Haight-Ashbury Clinic who was addicted to barbiturates at age ten and another who had aplastic anemia from sniffing glue at age seven. These are the drug users you're most likely to see with an acute drug reaction.

For the second category, I prefer the term "periodic" to "recreational" for the simple reason that the experimental user may also be out to have fun. The periodic user, however, has gone beyond the thrill of trying a new sensation and has settled into a pattern of use, not for pathological reasons but just to have a good time. His attitude is much like that of the social drinker, and like the social drinker, he may occasionally over-indulge. But he knows what the consequences will be and when they come, he gets through them without any help or with the help of his friends, because he's usually part of a subculture in which recreational drug use is as accepted as the cocktail party in the dominant culture. So you're not so likely to see the periodic user in your office.

But like the social drinker, he's also in some danger of passing into the next category. The compulsive drug user is the one who has gone beyond periodic or recreational use and feels a need for the drug, whether it's a true physical dependence or a psychological need. Usually he acquires a tolerance for his drug and begins increasing the dosage. This is when the acute reactions are likely to occur. But these patients are less likely than some of the other types of user to seek treatment because they are more concerned with concealing their compulsive use of drugs or because they don't recognize their use as compulsive. And you may fail to recognize it too.

In this group you may find the housewife or the businessman who takes off in the morning on two or three diet pills to create a kind of maintenance euphoria to counteract the boredom or tension of the day's tasks, and then comes down at night with barbiturates or a few drinks. Both patients and physicians often have a stereotyped vision of the drug user: He has long hair, he's a radical, and that's what a dope fiend is. It's hard to accept the fact that middle-class Mrs. Jones is also a dope fiend.

The ritualistic drug user takes drugs because he believes that they help him find some spiritual or religious experience. These users are not really germane to the discussion here because they don't usually have a drug abuse problem. Very often the ritualistic user eventually goes beyond drugs, stops taking them altogether, and develops a very personal, nonchemical turn-on.

These categories are by no means mutually exclusive. Obviously every drug user was once an experimental user. And those who use one drug periodically or compulsively may continue to experiment with other drugs. The individual who smokes pot occasionally for kicks may be compulsive in his use of amphetamine, and there is always the danger that either experimental or periodic use may lead to compulsive use.

David E. Smith, M.D., in article, "The Trip There and Back," from *Emergency Medicine*, December, 1969.

The Ubiquity of Harmful Substances

Even with the most carefully controlled environment there is the possibility of drug abuse if the individual is willing to experiment. George D. Scott, (*Drugs and Reality in Captive Society: Some Observations on Chemical Adaptation*, Canadian Psychiatric Association Journal. 15(2):215-222, 1970.) reports on the varieties of deadly chemicals prisoners have ingested as an escape from their reality. The list includes anything that has an alcohol evaporative quotient, inhalant ether, gasoline fumes, acetone, airplane glue, typewriter cleaner fluid, mice pellets with a strychnine content, mace and nutmeg, stick cologne and stick deodorant, perfume mixed with a carbonated drink, cake shoe polish melted and strained, mixed with orange juice, hair spray, nail polish remover, turpentine, and anything that will ferment.

Wyeth Laboratories, a manufacturer of pharmaceuticals, has released an informative little booklet, "The Sinister Garden," which illustrates nature's habit of producing beautiful and seemingly innocent, nevertheless deadly, lures. Examples which follow also show how difficult it is to say what things constitute "dangerous substances," the catchall phrase frequently used in place of the term "drugs."

. . ."Almost as if Nature had some sinister scheme, the most toxic parts of poisonous plants are usually the most attractive to children, who are prompted to experiment indiscriminately with roots, fruits, flowers and stems, whether they happen to enjoy their taste or not."

. . . MISTLETOE (Phoradendron). Toxic parts: berries.
Symptoms: Ingestion of the white berries or of "téas" brewed from berries has caused complete cardiovascular collapse and symptoms of acute gastroenteritis. Many cattle die yearly from eating the wild species of mistletoe growing on the coastal ranges of California. . .

POTATO (Solanum tuberosum). Toxic parts: Greenish spots on the tuber (edible portion), shoots, sprouts, leaves and stems.
Symptoms: Only the tuber of the potato is edible. Ingestion of the rest of the plant may cause mental confusion, cardiac depression and clammy skin. Has proved fatal. . .

NARCISSUS (Narcissus). Toxic part: Bulb.
Symptoms: Ingestion of bulbs of the narcissus family (including the daffodil and jonquil) can produce severe gastroenteritis, vomiting, trembling and convulsions which have led to fatalities. . .

CHERRY (Prunus). Toxic part: Twigs, leaves, bark and fruit stones.
Symptoms: Ingestion of all but the fruit of either wild or cultivated cherries can cause death within one hour with few outward signs of poisoning other than vertigo, spasms and finally, coma. The rapidity of the reaction is readily understood: the toxic part of the plant combines in the body to form cyanide.

From *The Sinister Garden*, Wyeth Laboratories.

Mistletoe (Phoradendron)

Potato   (Solanum tuberosum)

Narcissus (Narcissus)

Cherry (Prunus)

How, then, can we ever start to teach a child what is safe? Must practically everything he may find or touch become something to be cautioned against?

. . . One of the most often misused substances is aspirin. Each year it is involved in more than a quarter of the cases of accidental poisoning among children. With this in mind, the American Academy of Pediatrics is now voicing concern over reports that a double-strength, ten-grain aspirin product may soon be marketed. [Ed.—product now on market.] The academy is asking doctors to submit documented reports of any poisonings caused by the new dosage form, which, it says, "represents twice the poisoning hazard of the familiar 300-mg [five-grain] tablet."

"Household Agents Pack Deadly Punch," from *Medical World News*, **March 1, 1968.**

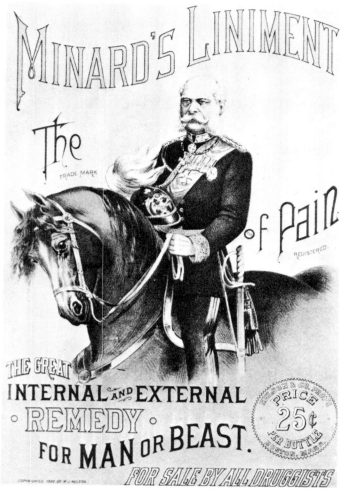

The Mystery of Pain

There is negligible mention of pain in the literature of drug abuse, despite the attention given the subject by the advertising and pharmaceutical companies and the fear and respect for pain felt by nearly all of us. The story of man's search for remedies for pain is a long one.

George A. W. Boehm recently reported that "a rapid accumulation of small discoveries and insights over the past four or five years suggests that the mastery of pain is an attainable goal for the 1970's." In his article, "Science Assaults Another Juggernaut: Pain," he states that

. . . Investigators of pain-relieving drugs have finally agreed on what they are attempting to measure and how to measure it. Only a few years ago, two leading clinics evaluating a new drug were almost as likely as not to arrive at conflicting conclusions about the effectiveness.

Safe methods of electrically stimulating certain regions of the brain have, in a few experiments, produced an aura of contentment little short of rapture, which completely overrides pain.

The degree to which a person suffers has been linked to such factors as sex, ethnic background, occupation and personality. Thus, there is hope that pain can be subtly and simply manipulated by psychology.

A theory explaining how nerve networks interact to blot out pain is now being refined. In its present state it hints at explanations of many of the enigmas of pain, and ultimately it may point the way to methods of relief radically different from any that have ever been tried.

. . . What, then, is the nature of pain? Throughout history philosophers have tried to define it, without notable success. Spinoza came closest to the modern scientific concept: he thought pain was a basic emotion equivalent to sharply focused sorrow. Then and now, language fails before pain's subtleties; few have found words descriptive or precise enough to explain its torments. As Virginia Woolf once wrote: "The merest schoolgirl, when she falls in love, has Shakespeare and Keats to speak for her; but let a sufferer try to describe a pain in his head to a doctor and language at once runs dry."

Scientists, too, have found that describing pain is an almost insuperable obstacle. A leading authority on the pathways of sensation within the human nervous system, W. J. H. Nauta of MIT, not long ago observed: "Pain is not anatomical. It is existential" —a state of the mind rather than a condition of the brain. One of the first scientists to anticipate this now generally-accepted view was the late W. K. Livingston, who more than twenty years ago founded a pain clinic at the University of Oregon. "I am unwilling to call anything pain unless it is perceived as such," he said. He had no patience with the then common notions that a fresh bullet wound emits "unfelt" pain, or that the throbbing of a phantom limb is "imaginary" pain. Pain, rather, is what a person says it is.

. . . Modern pain research has given physicians a much clearer idea of what drugs can accomplish.

The hope of miraculously enhancing pain relief by combining two or more drugs is now waning, although Houde has found that giving the usual dose of aspirin together with an equi-effective dose of codeine is generally more effective than doubling the dose of either drug alone.

Literally hundreds of narcotics have been synthesized and tested, but none is conspicuously better than morphine. For every narcotic there seems to be a "ceiling" dose, above which the patient is seriously imperiled by side effects—notably, interference with the breathing mechanism.

Some pain scientists believe that they will eventually be able to accomplish more through psychology than with drugs.

. . . The most potent measures for relieving pain hardly affect sensation, although they do banish concern. A person drugged with morphine admits he feels pain, but does not care. The same is true with electrically stimulated patients, with stoic Eskimos, with congenitally pain-blind children, and even with people who are too busy to worry about a toothache.

To Dr. Frank Ervin (Massachusetts General Hospital), this suggests that personal control of pain, perhaps without the use of drugs or electricity, is a definite possibility. He says: "We need to rationalize the anecdotal wisdom of the Yogis who can, in effect, "turn off" the burning coals and the spiky beds. Ultimately, we may be able to teach individuals how to control their pain by concentrating on it."

(Portions of article by George A. W. Boehm in *Think* Magazine, May-June, 1970.) Reprinted by permission from *Think* Magazine, published by IBM, Copyright 1970 by International Business Machines Corporation.

The prospect of the conquest of pain in the near future taxes one's credulity and may outweigh in importance mankind's longstanding difficulties with drugs. If it is hard to get agreement on definitions and ways for society to deal with dangerous substances, perhaps it is becoming clearer that the very considerable dangers of drug abuse probably will continue to be offset by much greater benefits.

The flight from discomfort, from whatever pain is, does not, by itself, explain why many people turn to drugs. The next chapter takes up the fundamental and baffling questions of why people take drugs and shows how exceedingly complex the reasons are.

Chapter Two

WHY PEOPLE TURN TO DRUGS

Early in our search of the literature, especially that concerned with the etiology of drug addiction, we were struck by the wide range of explanations as to why people use drugs to excess, and we took note of several (at least 24) factors commonly assumed to operate as causative influences. Many spokesmen champion a single factor or find themselves espousing somewhat contradictory causes. Every scheme to prevent drug abuse grows from and depends upon beliefs about the factors that lead to unhealthy or undesirable behavior.

Thus we found in both lay and professional writings a variety of sharply contrasting assumptions as to why people turn to drugs. In the illustrative list that follows, we have intensified the polarities in these beliefs somewhat by stressing age differences in behavior and attitudes related to drugs.

Some Contrasting Assumptions

- Young people do not have sufficient information about drugs.
  Young people know more than their teachers and parents about drugs.

- Young people put faith in unreliable sources of information.
  Adults must know all the facts, or the kids won't believe anything they say.

- Young people would rather learn about drugs from ex-addicts.
  Young people would rather learn about drugs from their trusted peers.

- Pushers persuade children to experiment with drugs.
  Children are persuaded to experiment by their friends.

- Law enforcement agencies lack the will and the resources to crack down on drug traffic and usually catch only the user-pusher.
  Law enforcement officers harass young people, particularly those with long hair.

- The laws are not tough enough; they do not instill enough fear.
  The laws are so tough and unfair as to encourage disobedience and reduce respect for lawmaking processes and society itself.

- Young people use drugs because they are so readily available.

  Young people delight in discovering and improvising upon any source of highs from shoe polish to nail lacquer remover, or anything else kept in the bathroom or under the kitchen sink.

- Young people refuse to listen; they hate to be lectured.

  Young people are overbearing moralists themselves.

- The drug problem started at home with the breakdown of family discipline and with drinking and pill-taking as parental examples.

  The drug problem was started and is maintained by Turkish, Mexican, French, and other foreign interests.

- The hopelessness of life in urban slums leads to drug dependence.

  The affluence and jaded quality of life in the suburbs leads to drug dependence.

- The credo of permissiveness in the schools causes students to feel that anything goes.

  The students are demoralized into drugs by an irrelevant curriculum and by coerciveness, archaism and depersonalization in the schools.

- Parental permissiveness leads to drug abuse.

  Parents are too demanding and strict, and force children to seek an inner freedom through drugs.

- Adolescents are self-indulgent and lack will-power.

  Adolescents have resolved to turn away from materialistic values at any cost, and they are determined to make a new world of their own.

- Narcotics are used by adolescents and young adults to gain relief from sexual and homosexual anxieties.

  Sexual freedom and hedonistic cultism lead to many kinds of thrill-seeking and especially to the exploration of hallucinogenic experiences.

- Young people are searching for deep, religious experiences, and unity with the universe.

  Young people have no respect for established religious practices and institutions and have no faith in the moral system of their parents.

Our list of contrasting assumptions clearly is not exhaustive. It does not deal with pain, for example, nor with basic experiences for older people, such as fears of death, failure, rejection, and loneliness. Highs probably bring comfort to weak egos and uncertain identities, and also to those who greatly disapprove of themselves.

It is safe to say therefore that much of the misunderstanding and many of the program failures in drug abuse education result from simplistic assignment of causes. Everybody has his own favorite explanation, including specialists such as psychiatrists who are apt to claim authoritative knowledge despite competition from others with comparable credentials. Perhaps the tendency of the experts to emphasize their favorite opinions on causation helps to explain the quarrelsomeness among research people and practitioners in fields associated with drug abuse. Though the following selections do not cover all the reasons an individual turns to drugs, we think that the complexities revealed in these brief excerpts will deepen your appreciation of the dilemmas in which the drug abuser and the drug specialist find themselves.

. . . The area of use and abuse of drugs is a good example of the role of biases, even among professionals. Specialists in each area look at the total problem and see it primarily from the perspective of their own theoretical background, major involvement and experience. Thus, the medically trained see in bold relief the medical aspects of the problem. But even within this one point of view, there are differences in emphasis depending on whether one's special interest is research or clinical practice, psychiatry, psychopharmacology or public health. The same can be said about the many other specialists who get into the act: the psychologists, sociologists, anthropologists, enforcement agents, social workers, ministers and journalists. Each one tends to ask different questions and to seek answers in different ways. It reminds one of the proverbial blind men and the elephant.

It is no wonder, then, that the layman, the legislator, the college administrator, the college student, faced with a multitude of points of view, resorts to selective perception, and chooses that position which does the least violence to his own established pattern of attitudes and beliefs. . . . One of the complicating factors is that adult patterns, having persisted for a longer time, tend to be more elaborate and more firmly held than those of college students.

Helen Nowlis in "Communicating About Drugs," from speech made at the National Association of Student Personnel Administrators Drug Education Conference, Wash., D.C., Nov., 1966, in the NIMH *Resource Book for Drug Abuse Education.*

Factors Contributing to Drug Abuse

A telling argument that drugs are used primarily to improve "feelings" has been advanced by A. J. Vogl in "Why Youngsters Take Drugs," *Medical Economics*, April 20, 1970. Finding in drugs a safe retreat from anger inside oneself may not seem *reasonable*, but the anger to be replaced or assuaged probably does not have a rational basis either. Abusers, Vogl contends, try to substitute "good feelings" for acute discomforts such as guilt, loneliness, and a painfully poor opinion of themselves. "Though misguided," Vogl points out, the person who "drugs for a social purpose is likely to be emotionally healthier than one who doesn't." Thus, the cocktail partygoer appears to be better off than the solitary drinker. "Those who use drugs to withdraw from social life . . . tend to be more disturbed and pathological," he concludes.

While the attraction of thrill and danger lead many to experiment with drugs, some permit the drug to assume a dominant role in their lives, obliterating all other aspects of living. The following factors can be isolated as a way of understanding why individuals flirt with and sometimes become captivated by drug abuse.

1) *Pleasure And Thrill Seeking Involves Flirting With Danger, Death And Destruction.* The actual acting upon death wishes in some extreme cases illustrates the literal carrying out of this wish, but far more subtle indications of this are present in the use of drugs that brings one to the borderline loss of self-boundaries and self-control.

2) *Gaining Status* with peers through demonstrating bravado and sophistication and *"Keeping Up With The Crowd"* are frequent introductions to drug abuse.

3) The *Defiance Of Authority* is an important aspect of the use of drugs, making it particularly appealing to those who are disillusioned with the adult generation.

4) *Sensual Stimulation* is particularly evident in the smoking of marijuana and glue sniffing. The direct tactile, olfactory, and auto-erotic aspects of these experiences are particularly intriguing to young adolescents who seek new sensations in their just beginning self-awareness.

5) *Low Frustration Tolerance* is frequently found in those who look to drugs as a way of obliterating anxiety. The quick, panacea-like experience produced by the drugs serves to dull unpleasant inner experiences.

6) *Escapism* is evident in the use of many of these agents which permit both psychological and physical removal of one's self from what is perceived as an unpleasant world. "Killing time" and alleviation of boredom through "blowing the mind" are provided by the drug.

7) The *Sense Of Alienation* experienced by many late adolescents today leads them to seek chemical stimulation as an organizing experience that gives temporary meaning and significance to life. The temporary 'breakthrough' provided by the drug experience APPEARS to satisfy wishes for intimacy, fusion and deep emotional involvement with others.

8) LSD-like agents in particular have developed around groups that use them for *Religious Purposes*. The Native American Church, an outgrowth of a Mexican-Indian religious movement, is an illustration of a large number of people who utilize peyote as a sensual instrument.

9) Some people seek drugs to *Enhance Aesthetic Appreciation Or Expression*. They may or may not be artists. These individuals especially seek to enjoy perceptual changes: increased vividness of color, visual harmonies, change in depth perception, sharper definition of details, and changes in time sense.

10) And mention should be made of those who seek to *Develop Cults* based upon the use of psychedelic agents for the purposes of fraud and extortion.

Frank K. Johnson, M.D. and Jack C. Westman, M.D., Department of Psychiatry, University of Wisconsin, in "The Teenager and Drug Abuse," *Journal of School Health*, Dec. 1968.

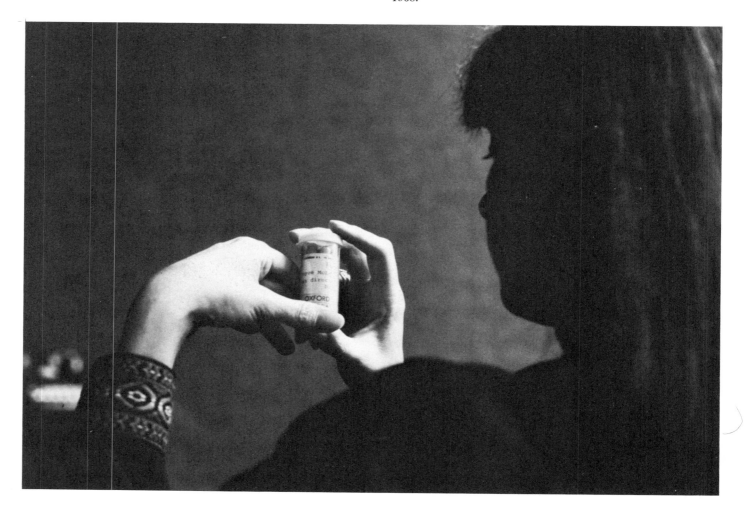

Graham Blaine divides causative factors of drug users into three categories—"the experience seekers," "the oblivion seekers," and "the personality-change seekers."

The "experience seeker" is an individual who either because of social pressures to experiment or because of a fascination with the dangers of arrest, addiction, or dying takes a limited number of forays into the drug culture. When queried about his experience, he will often ascribe some philosophic benefit to the experience rather than admit it was conformity that led him to experiment. Unless the experience seeker is unfortunate enough to suffer a lingering psychiatric state, the prognosis for this individual is good. Easy access to a concerned listener who is knowledgeable about drug effects and dangers, assistance in helping the patient define his own goals, and offering alternative outlets for energy (such as the Peace Corps, VISTA, and other volunteer projects) are useful techniques the pediatrician can utilize to help these young people. If the patient's motive is to shock his parents into becoming concerned, he may be successful by having his parents invest more of themselves in his case, or he may have to rely on another adult in the community for emotional support.

The "oblivion seeker" finds a drugged state a pleasant respite from the stresses of the world. He is more often chronically involved with drugs. Although purporting to resort to drugs because of the world's unpardonable injustices, many of these young people are actually burdened by feelings of incompetence and inadequacy. Considering that many of the dropouts are actually "left-outs" and "kick-outs," the pediatrician's role in these instances is primarily one of prevention. He can help prevent oblivion seeking if he can help parents of young children avoid making their children feel rejected and influence our educational system so efforts are directed not only toward applauding winners but also toward rewarding the pluggers. Once this syndrome has developed, these patients require somewhat prolonged help. The pediatrician's initial reaction may be one of despair, but he can be very helpful in a supportive role.

A helpful technique is to guide the adolescent in making a realistic inventory of his strengths, interests, and sources of conflict. Then, one can encourage progressive development in areas of potential. If, for example, the adolescent enjoys art, one can often muster community resources for giving him practical, noncompetitive experiences in the art classes, volunteer redecoration of a room, or working with a small group of elementary school children. Since the patient has probably been told all his life that he could do better if he "would only apply himself," he must be made to feel that this time he is striving for the goal of enhancement of his own self-esteem, not just to make his parents proud or to give his teachers the satisfaction of saying that they "were right all along—he could do much better."

If, in a realistic assessment of the patient's environment, it becomes apparent that he and his parents have reached an impasse in their relationship, it is sometimes helpful to remove the patient from his home. This move may be to another home in the community, a half-way house for troubled teenagers, or a social agency. Unfortunately, these resources are often more desirable than available, but churches and youth committees, for example, can cooperate in setting them up.

The third category, the "personality-change seeker," feels compelled to combine drugs and escalate dosages as his disappointment and frustration mount and as the "trade-in" personality he desires fails to materialize. He has an underlying basic personality problem, such as a character disorder. A major clue in these instances is that the young person's problems appear chronic. One has the sense that these individuals were very troubled even before they discovered drugs and that drugs have only added to their difficulties. Even with prolonged and intensive psychiatric therapy, the salvage rate is disappointingly low.

Graham Blaine, Chief of Psychiatry, Harvard University Student Health Services, in *I/D/E/A Occasional Paper: High School Students And Drugs*, 1970.

The following selections deal with an aspect of addiction that gets surprisingly little attention in studies of causation, considering the massive literature that exists on drug abuse in general. Authors, Yves J. Kron and Edward M. Brown, have pointed out the importance of the sexual dilemma in the lives of the addicts they studied and treated.

Narcotics addiction usually springs from an attempt to avoid sexual confusion. Normal narcotics use is undertaken for anesthesia from pain; narcotics abuse is used to relieve sexual anxiety. The habitual use of narcotics eliminates stimulation from biological needs, including sex, which would be experienced as painful. Among urban addicts observed, drug use often begins in the months following the first adolescent sexual attempts. The condition is determined by deep-rooted dependency upon and identification with the mother. The potential addict, torn between impulses toward incest and homosexuality, seeks an escape. . . .

Sexual identity is no longer a problem in the desexualized world of narcotics. In it, the individual destroys not only his sexual identity but his personal identity as well. His adolescent years have been a series of attempts and failures at being a man. But all these forays result in disappointing role-playing. He tries the "cool" life, he explores sexual experiences with both women and men, and he finds nothing because he has nothing to give. He never gives; he always looks for the magical gift which is never given. He feels more and more lonely, isolated, in an empty world.

At base, the narcotics addict is neither heterosexual nor homosexual. This is attested to not only by his final anesthesia from all sex, but also by the alternating sexual role he plays with other men and women. In no case are these relationships marked by real intimacy or giving on the addict's part; rather, his is the incessantly demanding role of a frustrated child. . . .

Recognition of the sexual factor in the etiology of drug addiction has suffered from cultural puritanism and from the wave of post-Victorian reaction to Freudian theory. Both professionals and the public find it difficult to assign sexuality any decisive role in its development. . . .

. . . The emphasis here on the importance of the sexual dilemma in addicts is derived, not from psychoanalytic preconceptions on the part of the authors, but from the evidence presented by addicts themselves.

In the course of his work with incarcerated addicts at Sing Sing prison, one of the authors, Yves Kron, M.D., made a systematic study in reference to their sex lives. Among the several hundred addicts examined and psychiatrically evaluated, he found that the first injection of heroin usually took place in the six months following the first heterosexual intercourse or attempt at intercourse. Addicts observed in out-patient treatment showed a similarly high correlation between onset of drug use and either recent sexual experimentation or crucial changes in the family constellation, such as death of the father. The uniformity of addicts' short-term marriages—if marriage takes place at all—and the high rate of homosexual prostitution further point to sexual confusion.

The Alksne study of adolescent addicts at Riverside Hospital showed that only one out of four addicts, while not using drugs, maintained a continuing relationship with one person of the opposite sex. This pattern of noninvolvement with members of the opposite sex is only one among many signs of the addict's difficulties with sexual feelings.

Biological evidence further supports this impression. Narcotics not only reduce pain and anxiety, but almost entirely eliminate the capacity for sexual responsiveness. In general, the urban addict begins narcotics use between the ages of fourteen and sixteen. If such use does not immediately follow puberty, it does occur at a time when dating or heterosexual experimentation begins. Addicts who begin using drugs at a later age show a better rate of improvement under treatment, as well as qualitatively different characteristics.

Several factors account for the sexual confusion evident among urban adolescents from low-income minority-group families. First, and most important, the incidence of family disintegration and of absentee fathers is high. Fatherless families have obvious economic troubles and are attracted to low-rent areas of large urban centers. Second, where male heads of households exist in potential addicts' families, they are usually not only inadequate passive fathers for their sons, but also unlikely competitors for wages. Third, overcrowded tenement apartments expose children to sexuality at an early age, so that stimulation and potential anxiety are heightened. Fourth, minority groups are pressed into the "inner city"; they suffer from role collision in employment, education, and family life, which magnifies the personal identity problem. Fifth, in a specific minority group, that of the Negro, the males, still only three generations from slavery, have been unable to find their own masculine image in a society which still insists upon treating them as inferior.

Sexual confusion is not assigned here as the only cause of narcotics addiction, but it is one of several complex causative factors and at the same time appears to be the crucial participating cause. The Alcoholism and Drug Addiction Research Foundation in Toronto describes the phenomenon as "reversed sexuality," and has built an experimental program around strengthening the sexual identity of its addict patients. Other observers call it the "masculine protest." We are inclined to emphasize the masculine denial, or under the full impact of narcotics, the general sexual denial.

The subject of sexuality in the problem of addiction has been considered by many current authorities in the field of narcotics addiction, but they have not expanded their observations. Marie Nyswander, one of the most prominent and astute psychiatrists involved in the treatment of addicts, has raised this issue; she has described the sexual inhibition in addicts at length, and has noted that when sexual experiences occur during periods of narcotics use, the addicts involved report that morphine enables them to engage in sexual relations without anxiety. Specifically, Dr. Nyswander has raised the question of whether sexual anxiety is the cause or a result of addiction.

The United States Public Health Service Hospital has engaged in a good deal of study on the pharmacology of narcotics addiction in a federal prison setting in Lexington, Kentucky. Abraham Wikler, widely recognized as a leading research neuropsychiatrist, has pointed out the relationship between narcotics and sex. One of his summaries clearly states the connection:

> On the basis of information obtained from the subjects themselves in psychiatric interviews it has been surmised that the "typical" narcotic addict is a passive, dependent type of psycopath who begins to "experiment" with various drugs during adolescence, and that his *initial* preference for heroin or morphine arises out of the unique ability of these narcotics to reduce all "primary" drives, notably those related to pain (in the sense of any type of physical discomfort) and sex—the latter being especially important in view of the emotional turmoil that this drive engenders during the adolescent period.
>
> . . . Because of the impracticality of conducting research on the sex drive in man, pain was selected as a model of a "primary" drive . . . it was shown that single doses of morphine (15 mg.) selectively reduce "anxiety associated with anticipation of pain" without impairing the ability to discriminate intensities of experimental pain. . . . The extent to which single doses of morphine affect "anxiety" associated with other "primary" drives is unknown, but analogous actions would not be inconsistent with the patient's description of their "indifference" to matters of sex, without loss of potency, when under the influence of morphine in the nontolerant state. (Abraham Wikler, "Psychologic Basis of Drug Abuse.")

One of the striking characteristics observed in working therapeutically with "inner city" families is their open approach to sexuality. The youngsters are much more familar with sexual experimentation than are their middle- and upper-class counterparts; exposure to sexual knowledge and immediate sexual experiences are not discouraged by adults, despite the conflict with mass-media mores, and the parents' confusion as to what behavior is appropriate. A fresh outlook, similar to the nonpunitive attitudes of these families, is now in order for the professional working with addicts, so that the precise role and pattern of sexuality in addiction can be further clarified. . . .

The addict's way of life is schizoid, a special kind of separation from the world. The early experiences in his life have been so fraught with danger and hurt that he adopts mechanisms of withdrawal for protection and for adaptation.

The schizoid position involves a minimum of three basic operations: blunting love, acquiring omnipotence, and fighting authority. Because the schizoid has found that love brings only pain, cannot be trusted, but only disappoints, he refuses to give any love and depersonalizes all individuals who offer closeness. He will denigrate any person who is loving toward him and attribute other motives to their gestures. Since he cannot trust anyone, he can rely only on his feelings, thoughts, and interpretations. He must make his own views absolute, unconditional, and omnipotent. Other viewpoints must be regarded as inferior.

Yves J. Kron, M.D. and Edward M. Brown, B.D. in *Mainline To Nowhere: The Making Of A Heroin Addict.*

Kron and Brown introduced their chapter on the female prostitute addict with a quote from a female patient, "There was no significant person in my life."

In establishing a sexual identity, both sexes have problems in the absence of a model, but the female has a special problem, according to the next reading, which explains why female addicts are usually more difficult to work with in therapy than male addicts.

. . . Not all prostitutes are drug addicts, but most female drug addicts are prostitutes. Every prostitute functions emotionally, if not sexually, at a homosexual level.

Most of these women are homosexuals first, inadequately identified as women and hostile toward men. Their prostitution, which comes second, fulfills their need to play a dominant role over men. Finally, they are addicts. While sometimes chronological case histories show that their use of drugs has emerged before the other characteristics, further examination will often indicate that latent signs of the homosexuality and subsequent prostitution had appeared in disguised form before the addiction. Such women often will have related socially to men in ways for which they have been paid or rewarded. As a girl, such a women might not have accepted a date with a boy unless he promised to buy her something in return. Later, she might have justified any intimacy by the material benefit it would bring: an expensive dinner or the gift of a new dress might have obtained her sexual cooperation. Relationships such as these are apt to begin earlier in adolescence for these women than comparable ones in the development of others. The sexual preoccupation is often evident in pre-teen-age years.

Addiction among women presents its own very special pattern of evolution, which makes it in many respects quite a different problem from its male counterpart. The preaddiction period in girls is usually of longer duration than that in men; most females become addicted through contact with male addicts. Out of a need for rebellion against male authority, they often engage in precocious sexual activity in which they find no sexual gratification. Their association with addicts, who are inadequate males, fulfills their unconscious desire to reject the male partner; men are an object of competition, not of sexual attraction. . . .

The female addict likes to dress as a man. Her relationship with men is a castrating one: she has no desire for men to be potent, because sexual acceptance of the man will make her feel inferior to him, or rather make her aware of her basic feeling of inferiority.

There is one outstanding difference between male and female addicts which takes its form in the habit itself. Women use cocaine to counter the emotional withdrawal and apathy caused by heroin. Cocaine incites a certain degree of elation which allows sexual activity.

This brief description of the female addict can be only a very general one, for the area of female addiction and its sexual confusion still suffers from limited investigation and insufficient research. More studies of female addicts are needed, as well as even greater understanding of the female personality itself as emancipated from a male-dominated culture. . . .

When girls do not adjust to their accepted social function, they seem to demonstrate their pattern of maladjustment more rigidly than boys, and this pattern appears more deeply ingrained in their personalities, which seem to become more distorted than those of their male counterparts. Boys are the victims of a missing feature, namely, identification with a father; although girls can identify with the mother, she is too often an inadequate woman who has transmitted a distorted role to her daughter. The inadequate mother has a worse effect on her children than do the circumstances created by a missing mother; a substitute may be found for the missing mother, but the inadequate mother serves as a destructive example.

Female addicts are even more difficult to reach therapeutically than their male counterparts. On the other hand, girls are better equipped for sheer emotional survival because of their identification, however faulty, with the mother. But when the mothers reject their daughters, not only the biological inheritance of the mothering role but also the feeling of not being loved reduces the daughter's capacity for finding a place in society. The characteristic inadequacies of the mother of the male addict are recognized, but the mother of the female addict appears not only inadequate but emotionally fragmented, lacking both a self-image and a feeling of purpose. . . .

Women who deviate from the sexual norm undergo reprobation, but confront much less hostility than men who do so. For women, homosexuality and even transvestism carry few legal consequences, and prostitution brings only mild penalty from the law.

Yves J. Kron, M.D. and Edward M. Brown, B.D. in *Mainline To Nowhere: The Making Of A Heroin Addict.*

There may be special causative factors at work in dependency upon certain classes of drugs, such as alcohol. In this country there are more people abusing alcohol than any other drug. Some people rightly feel that the danger of alcohol is being overlooked in the rush to find solutions for narcotics addiction, when so much needs to be known about the age-old problem of alcoholism. Theories abound to explain man's thralldom to fermented fruits and grains, but one of the most effective organizations helping people to abstain from alcohol, Alcoholics Anonymous, asks that its members start their testimonials by simply stating, "I am an alcoholic," followed by a statement of how long it has been since he or she last had a drink. What is an alcoholic, if one can remain such for years after ceasing to drink alcohol? Would it be helpful for a person to know that he is an alcoholic *before* he takes his first drink? And would he then take that drink? Robert F. Bales cites the following:

The effective motivation of the individual at any given time may be considered as the outcome of two sets of influences: the needs or urges which he carries within himself, and the opportunities which he finds in his situation. . . .

This account might be simplified by saying that there are three general ways in which culture and social organization can influence rates of alcoholism. The first is *the degree to which the culture operates to bring about acute needs for adjustment, or inner tensions, in its members.* There are many of these; culturally induced anxiety, guilt, conflict, suppressed aggression, and sexual tensions of various sorts may be taken as examples. The second way is *the sort of attitudes toward drinking which the culture produces in its members. . . .* The crucial factor seems to be whether a given attitude toward drinking positively suggests drinking to the individual as a means of relieving his inner tensions, or whether such a thought arouses a strong counteranxiety. The third general way is *the degree to which the culture provides suitable substitute means of satisfaction.* In other words, there is reason to believe that if the inner tensions are sufficiently acute certain individuals will become compulsively habituated in spite of opposed social attitudes unless substitute ways of satisfaction are provided.

Mr. Bales also gives four social attitudes toward alcohol:

The first is an attitude which calls for *complete abstinence.* For one reason or another, usually religious in nature, the use of alcohol as a beverage is not permitted for any purpose. The second might be called a *ritual attitude* toward drinking. This is also religious in nature, but it requires that alcoholic beverages, sometimes a particular one, should be used in the performance of religious ceremonies. Typically the beverage is regarded as sacred, it is consecrated to that end, and the partaking of it is a ritual act of communion with the sacred. . . . The third can be called a *convivial attitude* toward drinking. Drinking is a "social" rather than a religious ritual, performed both because it symbolizes social unity or solidarity and because it loosens up emotions which make for social ease and good will. . . . The fourth type seems best described as a *utilitarian attitude* toward drinking. This includes medicinal drinking and other types calculated to further self-interest or exclusively personal satisfaction. It is often "solitary" drinking, but not necessarily so. . . .

Robert Freed Bales in "Cultural Differences in Rates of Alcoholism," from *Deviant Behavior and Social Process.*

Why Children Turn to Drugs

Dr. Donald Kanter served as special consultant for the Coronado Unified School District (Calif.) Title III program with the mission to develop reliable information upon which to prepare a K-12 curriculum approach which would give students skill in recognizing advertising strategies.

Dr. Kanter's initial research with hundreds of students clearly indicates that a number of commonly held opinions on the directly harmful influence of advertising upon youth indeed are supported only indirectly by his data.

. . . There is no doubt . . . that there is a relationship between drug use and certain kinds of advertising. However, this relationship is not the one which I expected going into the research.

The nature of the relationship is complex:

(1) Drug and cigarette advertising affects the very young (subteens) and encourages them to experiment with certain palliatives.
(2) Experimenting takes the form of increasing dosage, to see what kind of a kick can be obtained.
(3) Pleasure and relief is depicted in many advertisements, particularly drug and cigarette commercials. These depictions of relief and personal satisfaction act as reinforcing agents to general teen-age usage.
(4) Teen-age *initial* experimenting and drug advertising do not seem directly related; but early usage of excessive aspirin, Midol, etc., could be the seedbed for later experimentation.

. . . to ignore advertising's reinforcing function in the general world of the teen-ager as well as the sub-teen seems also incorrect. . . .

Dr. Donald Kanter, Professor of Consumer Psychology, University of Southern California. From 1969 interim report on "Advertising Media Influence On Drug Abuse And Countering Education Program," by Coronado Unified School District.

Young people not only have to work out an adequate sexual identity, they also have to gain experience in an adolescence and school environment prolonged far beyond the date for growing up assigned to their counterparts in earlier times. Kenneth Keniston, Associate Professor of Psychiatry, Yale University, discusses the pressures, the clashing values of today. The most visible pressures on today's students, Dr. Keniston contends, go against the young person's need for intense personal experiences to help him find the meaning of life.

The Search for Meaning

Among today's self-conscious students, the statement, "I'm having an identity crisis" has become a kind of verbal badge of honor, a notch in the gun, a scalp at the belt. But although the term 'identity crisis' can be easily parodied and misused,

it points to fundamental issues of adolescence in all societies that are particularly heightened in our own society. Since academic pursuits, on the whole, tell the student so little about life's ultimate purposes, students are turned back upon their own resources to answer questions like, "What does life mean? What kind of a person am I? Where am I going? Where do I come from? What really matters?" . . .

The Cult of Experience

The cult of experience has often been discussed as a defining characteristic of American youth cultures. Central to this cult is a focus on the present —on today, on the here-and-now. Thus, rather than defer gratifications and enjoyment for a distant future, immediate pleasure and satisfaction are emphasized. Rather than reverence for the traditions of the past, experience in the present is stressed. Psychologically, then, such human qualities as control, planning, waiting, saving, and postponing on the one hand, and revering, recalling, remembering and respecting on the other, are equally deemphasized. In contrast, activity, adventure, responsiveness, genuineness, spontaneity and sentience are the new experimental values. Since neither the future nor the past can be assumed to hold life's meaning, the meaning of life must be sought within present experience, within the self, within its activity and responsiveness in the here-and-now.

Disaffiliation and Drugs

. . . My own experience with student drug-users convinces me that there are many different motives for drug use and abuse, and there are many different factors—psychological, sociological, cultural and situational—that determine whether one student will use drugs while another will not. But despite the diversity of student types who may become involved in drug use, there is, I believe, one type that is particularly prone to drug abuse. I will call such students 'disaffiliates,' and will summarize some of the factors that predispose these students toward drug abuse. The defining characteristic of the disaffiliate is his generalized rejection of prevalent American values, which he rejects largely on esthetic, cultural and humanistic grounds. Such students are rarely political activists, and they are rarely concerned with the issues of economic, social and political justice that agitate many of their classmates. For these students, the problem is not political or social, but esthetic: American society is ugly, trashy, cheap and commercial; it is dehumanizing; its middle-class values are seen as arbitrary, materialistic, narrow and hypocritical. Thus, those conventional values which deem experimentation with drugs—or experimentation of all kinds—illicit, are strongly rejected by disaffiliates; for them, what matters is somehow to seek a way out of the 'air conditioned nightmare' of American society.

A second characteristic of disaffiliates is a more or less intense feeling of estrangement from their own experience. Such students are highly aware of the masks, facades and defenses people erect to protect themselves; and not only do they criticize these defenses in others, but even more strongly in themselves. These feelings of estrangement are often accompanied by considerable depression and a strong sense of personal isolation. Indeed, depression following the loss of an important relationship is commonly found in the immediate background of the student who begins to abuse drugs. For the student with intensified feelings of estrangement from himself and others, drugs that promise to heighten experience seem a tempting way out of his shell.

A third relevant characteristic of disaffiliates is a fantasy of fusion and merger, which contrasts sharply with their current feelings of estrangement. In the background, many of these students have a concept of an almost mystical fusion with nature, with their own inner lives, or above all with other people—a kind of communication that requires no words, a kind of oneness with nature or the world that has characterized intense religious experience for centuries, a special kind of automatic oneness with another. For an undergraduate with an especial longing for oneness with others, the hallucinogens are especially tempting. For one characteristic of the drug experience is a weakening or breaking down of the boundaries of the self such that many individuals in fact report feelings of oneness, merger and fusion with others.

Kenneth Keniston in his paper, "Drug Use and Student Values," presented at National Association of Student Personnel Administrators Drug Education Conference, Washington, D.C., Nov., 1966, from NIMH *Resource Book for Drug Abuse Education.*

Graham Blaine has summarized some of the forces that influence boys and girls of junior high and high school age to take drugs:

1. To prove their courage by indulging in risk-taking
2. To act out their rebellion and hostility toward authority
3. To facilitate sexual desires and performance
4. To elevate themselves from loneliness and provide an emotional experience, or,
5. To attempt to find the meaning of life.

In I/D/E/A *Occasional Paper: High School Students and Drugs* (1970), he says, "It is essential to recognize that there is no such thing as a completely stereotyped user. Rather, each user is unique as to his experiences and constitution. Those who use drugs are not necessarily alienated or in rebellion or even emotionally disturbed, though they may be. Each case must be judged individually."

Why do teenagers turn to drugs in the first place? We all realize that we're living in a drug-oriented society. We hear so much on television that my three-year old knows the Bufferin and Anacin commercials by heart and is beginning to ask me, "What does 'regularity' mean, Daddy?"

When we get sick, we go to the doctor for a shot of penicillin, knowing full well that the penicillin isn't going to touch the virus of a cold. It's been estimated that the average American uses from three to five mind-altering drugs each day—starting with the caffeine in his morning coffee through the nicotine in his cigarette, the diet pill, tranquilizers, sleeping pills, and alcohol. Just think about it. Just look into your medicine cabinet. You know children are great imitators. When they see a medicine cabinet lined with just about everything in the pharmacy, they begin to pick up the same feeling that so many adults have, that somehow drugs can be the answer to everything.

Ira Frank, M.D., Neuropsychiatric Institute, University of California, in "Psychedelic Drug Abuse Among Our Youth."

From *Drug Addiction and Drug Abuse*, June, 1969. (Selected Papers of a Seminar for Wyoming Physicians, Western Interstate Commission for Higher Education, Boulder, Colorado.)

. . . drugs are fun. In the authors' interviews with teen-age users the most common response to the question of "Why?" was, "It's fun!" In spite of the Protestant Ethic, there has developed in America a pleasure-seeking ethos. . . .

Next comes sensuality. This is really a sub-category of "fun," but a very special one. We mentioned above that the senses of touch and taste have been very neglected in our culture. Therefore the exploration of them provides a special fascination for young people. Almost every marihuana party, and many LSD trips, involve a period when everyone gets the "hungries" and explores as wide a variety of taste delights as is available. More crucial, however, is the increase in cutaneous sensitivity, because one aspect of this is sexual stimulation. Our inquiries have not revealed much interest in sex during LSD trips. There is no doubt, however, that teen-agers have discovered that pot makes the exploration of sex more delightful. As far as we can tell, this has not meant an increase in sexual exploitation or carelessness. The hippies, whom the mass media use to create this kind of impression, seem to have been emotionally disturbed and sexually rebellious before dropping out into the drug subculture.

The problem, it seems, is that teen-agers are more permissive about both drugs and sex than are older generations, so that it is easy to read into the situation a causal connection that is not necessarily there. There is a generational change that parents themselves have helped to create. Today, parents themselves, although sometimes unwilling to admit it, are more permissive about sex and sensuality than they were 20 years ago. . . .

Winfield W. Salisbury, Ph.D., and Frances R. Fertig, B.A., Department of Sociology, San Jose State College, San Jose, Calif., in "The Myth of Alienation and Teenage Drug Use: Coming of Age in Mass Society," from California School Health, Winter, 1968. NIMH Resource Book for Drug Abuse Education.

An unlooked for, and to some surprising, conclusion is that medical care of high quality can lead to misplaced faith in drugs and an attitude of optimism about the effects of drugs, which, in turn, can lead to drug dependency. Dr. Richard H. Blum, Director, Psychopharmacology Project, Institute for the Study of Human Problems, Stanford University, has come to the following conclusion:

A problem rarely mentioned and which we must call attention to when we accept our premise of expanding drug use, is the role of physicians in contributing to the expanded use. From our pilot survey we have some evidence that the people who became exotic drug users, and this tends to be a well-educated young sample in a normal population, had larger exposure to medical care. Their parents had been more interested in giving them drugs, they had been taken to the doctor more often when they were kids, and they learned to take drugs. They had become drug optimists, if you will, and I suspect many of us are drug optimists. We give a great vote of confidence to the pharmaceutical industry and to modern medicine. So we should not overlook the role of the physician as an instructor in drug use. We believe we can control our insides with these little capsules. It is a very simple belief—yet its ramifications are immense. How could we expect our children not to take drugs if this is what we have taught them?

Richard H. Blum, Ph.D., in Drugs and Personal Values, paper presented at National Association of Student Personnel Administrators Drug Education Conference, Washington, D.C., Nov., 1966. NIMH Resource Book for Drug Abuse Education.

Some drug use in school presumably stems from disaffection with the educational process. An interview with one student, reported by the National Institute of Mental Health, illustrates this. Asked, "Do many kids go to school stoned?" The student's reply was "Yes." The next question was, "Doesn't this impair your efficiency in school?" The answer, "Of course." After that, "Well, why do you do it?" His answer was, "I wouldn't be able to stand school any other way."

With so many reasons advanced by people for taking some kind of palliative, is it any wonder that so little progress has been made toward stopping over-indulgence in certain medications and beverages, which, when used appropriately, have a place in our lives.

Also standing in the way of progress in the prevention of drug abuse are certain obstinate beliefs, and patterns of behavior that we have called myths, half-truths and mistakes, the title for our next chapter.

Chapter Three

MYTHS, HALF-TRUTHS AND MISTAKES

To deserve the name, a myth should contain a slice of truth about man and the world, but the word is used in this body of readings to connote easy answers to questions that require new answers, perhaps in the direction of new concepts about human nature. We do not mean "half-truths" as a derisive term, since a half-truth is logically better than no truth at all. Mistakes, surely, need no definition, though perhaps they are too much regretted. In the world of drugs people speak in strong language and often judge harshly. Without mistakes, we might not even have half-truths. In choosing among mistakes common to many laymen and professionals, we are aware that mistakes we can see so clearly today carried authority only yesterday and may seem charmingly innocent tomorrow. Meanwhile, in the name of discovering new techniques for new situations, we may be slighting the validity still to be tested in half-truths.

Advances in knowledge about drugs may be hard to discern and may seem to be happening largely through error and human suffering. Never-theless the process of learning continues, and it appears that people of all ages and kinds in many countries are learning a great deal about drugs. Hence, in terms of present understanding of the psychosocial aspects of drug dependence, these caveats may be worth mentioning, even though they are judgmental, especially alongside some of the sharply critical commentaries which follow.

Some Myths of Drug Addiction

One of the great myths of the day is that if a child goes wrong, becomes a drughead, for example, this must be due to parental failure. If the cause is not deprivation or neglect, it must be over-protection or possessiveness. At times it appears that the line between insufficient mothering and material smothering is nonexistent. This peculiar notion stems from the strong lay and professional indoctrination with the Freudian tenet that what happens in infancy determines subsequent behavior. The parents uncritically accept this thesis, and of course their children are quite willing to appropriate and elaborate on the theme that they received either too much or too little family love.

Unquestionably, substantial numbers of children are maltreated, abused, overcontrolled, or spoiled. This does not mean that they are completely incapable of overcoming these childhood handicaps. It would be both harmful and incorrect to believe that maladaptive personality patterns cannot be corrected. The individual has some responsibility in such matters. In addition, a large group of quite well-brought-up, characterologically sound children are "turned on" to drugs by their associates. It is difficult to discern how a parent can be blamed for these events. Sometimes, the parents are in a double bind. If they try to intervene, they are domineering; if they do not, they are neglectful.

Sidney Cohen, M.D., in *The Drug Dilemma.*

Dr. Donald Louria has identified in *Nightmare Drugs*, a dozen myths that seem to persist despite contrary facts.

Myth 1: Drug Addicts Frequently Commit Violent Crimes

The Fact. Persons addicted to opiates including morphine, demerol, and heroin are no more inclined to crimes of violence than the general population. Indeed, evidence suggests that those habituated or addicted to opiates are actually less likely to commit crimes of violence than others *in their environments.* This statement is supported by the official crime figures of the City of New York in 1964, and the 1965 figures are very similar. Statistics show that neither rape nor felonious assault are found more frequently among addicts. And while the 1964 figures on murder seem to bear out the blaring headlines each time a murder is attributed to a "dope fiend," the most that can be claimed is that murder *may* be slightly more frequent among addicts. Addicts are con men, liars, and thieves. They are generally not violent, either by nature or as a result of drug use. When they do commit violent crimes, it is frequently because of argu-

ments over narcotics with pushers or other addicts. In 1965 twenty-three of the thirty-two homicides by narcotics users in the City of New York were related to altercations over narcotics.

It should be emphasized that this applies to heroin and other opiates, but not to cocaine which is often associated with aggressive or violent behavior. Fortunately, as we indicated earlier, cocaine habituation is rare in the United States.

Myth 2: Drug Addicts Are Sex Fiends

The Fact. The administration of heroin or other opiates almost uniformly reduces sex urges. The habitué or addict usually remains potent but loses sex drive and inclination. Although cocaine produces aggressive behavior, it is not a sexual stimulant. Its action is short lived and the high is often felt by the taker as a feeling of intense sexual gratification which may act as a replacement for overt sexual activity.

Similarly, amphetamine and barbiturates may be taken at parties at which there is excessive sexual activity, but there is no evidence that either of these drugs is a sexual stimulant. On the other hand, the hallucinogens, especially LSD, may be stimulants for some persons; for most individuals, they are intellectual aphrodisiacs without a physical counterpart. That is, the content of the thoughts and hallucinations may be intensely erotic in nature, but the user does not usually turn from this mental stimulation to attempt to achieve physical gratification.

Myth 3: Pushers Actively Attempt to Entice the Uninitiated into Drug Abuse and Are Responsible for Its Spread

The Fact. Heroin pushers are parasites who supply drugs at an enormous profit, but only infrequently attempt to convert nonusers. Instead, they obtain the drugs and stand ready to sell heroin, sedatives, or pep pills to anyone who has the money to pay for them. Transactions today are cash first; users either carry the drug away with them or pick it up at a specified spot later. Drug addiction spreads from user to user, and the pushers, 80 per cent of whom are users themselves, merely stand ready in the wings to keep the evil cycle going by supplying the illegal drugs. The image of the pusher standing in a school yard urging the kids to take drugs is just not correct. Recent evidence in New York City, however, suggests that pushers of marijuana are becoming more aggressive in urging high school children to smoke pot.

Myth 4: Once You Take a Shot of Heroin, Addiction Is Inevitable

The Fact. There are large numbers of heroin users who use the drug only once or twice a week for many years, never becoming truly addicted. Among those who do become addicted, the time interval between the first mainline injection of the drug and addiction (defined as physical dependence) ranges from two weeks to one year. This is in part due to the fact that the drug is so adulterated by the time it reaches the street that it is difficult to become physically addicted in a short period of time.

Myth 5: Those Who Chronically Use Marijuana or Opiates Such as Heroin and Morphine Experience Progressive Physical Deterioration

The Fact. Physical deterioration from marijuana is virtually unheard of in this country, although it is thought to occur in countries where larger amounts or more potent forms of *Cannabis* are used. The physical deterioration that accompanies the illicit use of heroin is related not to the heroin or morphine itself but rather to personal neglect and the intravenous injection of unsterile material. It is almost certain that if needles were adequately sterilized, liver damage and infections of the heart valves would not occur. In short, physical deterioration frequently accompanies the illegal use of opiates, but this is due to unsanitary conditions rather than to adverse effects of the drugs themselves.

Myth 6: Abrupt Withdrawal ("Cold Turkey") Is a Reprehensible Act of Cruelty Towards Addicts Practiced Primarily by Law Enforcement Officials

The Fact. Nobody in any position of authority advocates cold turkey treatment of narcotics addicts. Nevertheless, the overwhelming majority of those using heroin today can be readily treated by cold turkey or by the administration of small amounts of sedatives or tranquilizers for a short period of time, without any harm. Ironically, thanks to the greed of the importers, sellers, and distributors of heroin, by the time the drug is purchased by the addict, it is so adulterated that even persons with $20- to $40-a-day habits may have no significant withdrawal symptoms on stopping the drug. A large proportion of those who claim they are addicted are, in fact, hooked on the needle or psychologically addicted but not physically dependent on the drug.

This is well illustrated by a patient who had a $30-a-day habit. She was promptly withdrawn in the hospital with no medication and had virtually no symptoms at all. When this was pointed out to her, she acknowledged that she could not have been truly addicted. Since she had indicated that she desperately wanted to discontinue the use of heroin, she was asked why she did not just stop the drug by herself, since she was not physically dependent upon it. She answered that she had heard terrifying stories of the horrors of sudden withdrawal. She knew it began with a runny nose. Every time she did not get a shot for several hours, her nose would itch and would begin to run slightly. Undoubtedly, her "addiction" was purely psychological, but the runny nose convinced her that she would soon have terrible withdrawal symptoms and she would therefore take another shot of heroin. It was not until she was in the hospital and all drugs were abruptly discontinued that she realized she could have stopped any time she wanted to.

As a matter of fact, a survey of hospitals with detoxification units indicates that it is now fairly easy to withdraw addicts from heroin, using nothing, just sedatives, or, in the more severe cases, methadone, over a short period of time. The problem is that many heroin addicts are also addicted to barbiturates, and withdrawal from these drugs is much more difficult and far more prolonged. The knowledge that severe physical dependence on heroin is now relatively infrequent invalidates the claim of many pushers that they are selling merely to support their habit. In some cases this may be true on a physical level; in others they are supporting a psychological addiction. Still others are using this rationalization to justify their continuing a heinous illicit drug traffic, and to disguise the real motivation, the extraordinary profits involved in illicit narcotics sale.

Myth 7: Narcotics Addiction Is a Medical Illness Similar to Diabetes

The Fact. Diabetes and similar diseases are illnesses in which the body cannot produce adequate amounts of a normal enzyme or hormone such as insulin and the body must therefore receive it from the outside. At a medical level, narcotic addiction can be compared only to other forms of drug overdose, and the treatment of drug overdose of any sort is to withdraw the drug. Comparing narcotic addiction to hormone deficiency is incorrect, confusing, and unjustified.

Myth 8: Narcotics Addiction Is a Contagious Disease

The Fact. A contagious disease is one which any individual who is not immune to the infection will acquire when exposed to it. It is nonsensical to compare addiction to a virus or infectious disease. Narcotic addiction is contagious in that users give drugs to those who want to try it, or in the sense that if one group in a neighborhood uses narcotics, it is likely that others will want to try it, either on their own or as a part of the group. This is sociologic contagion, but it has no relationship at all with a contagious medically infectious disease. If it were a true contagious disease, then practically 100 per cent of persons in neighborhoods where narcotics are illicitly used would become involved, and there is no evidence that this occurs.

Myth 9: Narcotic Addiction Is Basically a Medical Illness, but Doctors Will Not Get Into the Field Because of Persecution and Prosecution by the Legal Authorities

The Fact. The illicit use of narcotic drugs such as heroin becomes a medical problem when the individual develops complications such as overdose, liver disease, and heart valve infection. It becomes a medical problem during the time the individual is withdrawn from the narcotic after being physically addicted. But there is a great question as to whether or not narcotic addiction itself is basically a medical illness.

As noted before, there is no evidence at all that addicts have any innate physical drive to misuse drugs. Rather, their use of drugs seems to be an antisocial act directed against society or their families. The evidence is overwhelming that the majority of illicit drug users, at least those taking opiates and cocaine, have participated in antisocial, delinquent activities *before* turning to drugs. Thus, in its inception, narcotic addiction is, in the majority of cases, a sociologic disease.

There is meager evidence to suggest that doctors are not participating in the narcotics field because they are afraid of doing so. In point of fact, the narcotics addict is generally a difficult, demanding, unappreciative patient who does not really want to give up his drug use, and the majority of doctors in private practice have no inclination to become involved in this perplexing and, for the most part, unproductive field. In recent years, the only doctors prosecuted by law have been those committing outrageous acts, such as wholesale dispensing of unneeded prescriptions for a price, or outright sale of narcotics to addicts for a profit. Even those who have experimented with various forms of maintenance treatment against the letter of the law have not been arraigned by Federal or local authorities, although some have been told they must desist from such treatment unless they obtain official sanction for this experimental therapy.

It is true that when doctors request information they are told they must not maintain an addiction and must treat with withdrawal. Clarification of this ruling is clearly needed, but aside from this mild intimidation based on a rather stringent interpretation of Supreme Court decisions, there is no persecution of physicians. As long as physicians are unsure that narcotic addiction is primarily a medical problem, as long as they know that their attempts to help the addict on an outpatient basis will fail in the overwhelming majority of cases, and as long as they recognize that the addict is an extraordinarily difficult and unreliable patient, it will continue to be difficult to recruit physicians to this area of endeavor except in institutional and research settings.

Myth 10: Drug Addicts Have Specific Personality Defects

The Fact. Most addicts are immature hedonists, unable to tolerate frustration, angry against society, and unable to establish long-range goals. But only a minority, perhaps 10 per cent, are truly psychotic.

The rest fall into the catch-all categories of maladjusted personalities or sociopaths. There is no personality defect indigenous to addicts which does not occur among people not taking drugs. . . . Psychotherapy and psychiatric treatment have roles to play in the treatment of addiction, but the accumulated evidence indicates that unless treatment is accompanied by general rehabilitation, they will be successful only in a small number of cases.

Myth 11: Marijuana Is An Aphrodisiac Which Leads to Heroin Use and Results in Crime
This . . . is included here only for purposes of emphasis.

The Fact. Marijuana itself does not increase sex drive; it does release inhibitions, just as alcohol does, and because of this, it may increase attempts to obtain sexual gratification. Just as often, it reduces sex drive. In the United States, there is no evidence that the use of marijuana results in criminal activity. In other countries, where *Cannabis* is used to excess and the preparations are more potent, there does appear to be a correlation between excessive *Cannabis* intake and subsequent criminal activity. Although it is true that most heroin users have had prior experience with marijuana, it is also true that the overwhelming majority of those who try marijuana on one or more occasions never turn either to heroin or to stronger hallucinogenic agents.

Myth 12: Once an Addict, Always an Addict

The Fact. Although it is generally believed that once a person becomes addicted to narcotics he will remain so the rest of his life, and even if abstinent for a short period of time will eventually go back, this is clearly not true. As of 1964, only 11.7 per cent of the addicts known to the Federal Bureau of Narcotics were over the age of forty, and these figures reflect the experience of virtually everyone dealing with addicts. . . .
For a variety of reasons, addicts in their late thirties and early forties appear to lose their need for the drug. Often there is a beneficial change in their life situation: marriage, having children, moving to another neighborhood, or obtaining steady employment. As a result, motivation improves, and the addict voluntarily gives up his drugs. In other cases, the reasons are less apparent, but the phenomenon of "maturing out" seems to be valid and is well recognized by the addict himself. The concept of "Once an addict, always an addict," is specious; it is perpetuated both by those who are unaware of the life cycle of the addict, and by the young addict himself as a rationalization for returning to drugs after a period of voluntary or compulsory abstinence.

From "The Drug Scene," in *Nightmare Drugs* by Donald Louria, M.D.

So much has been said and written on the subject of the pusher, that we bring up the subject to show the fallacies in searching for scapegoats. Getting rid of pushers ranks high on the agenda of most programs designed to fight drug abuse. There are often heated arguments about just who the pusher is—he is sometimes a user-provider, who sells just enough to break-even on his habit; others have a certain life style to support, and are not gracious in extending credit or doing favors for friends.
The small-time pusher is the one, according to a broad section of opinion, that the law enforcement people are bright and brave enough to catch.
One way to detect people's biases is to listen to their definitions and descriptions of a pusher, most of which fall into stereotypes. One common characteristic of the pusher, according to much material still in circulation, is that he entices youngsters to take drugs, usually starting them off on the softer ones, and leading them on to the addictive drugs. But users have talked frequently about how they started sniffing, popping, puffing, dropping and shooting, and seldom is the pusher to blame.

A check-up session at Father Daniel Egan's Village Haven in New York, the therapeutic residence for female addicts, disclosed that of six girls taking part in discussion, all had been introduced to drugs, usually marijuana at the start, by friends. (One girl of 18 [years old] had started on pot as a member of a group of seven close friends, two now dead through hard-drug overdosing.)

None of those questioned had been "started" on drugs by professional pushers. It is rare to find an addict who was. Hard to face [is] that there is something of a "drug culture," in which the unhappy and lonesome seek each other out, and share a means of avoiding reality. It seems neater to blame the pusher, jumping out from a tree, supposedly, and introducing an adolescent to the use of drugs. This does happen in some ghetto areas, rarely elsewhere. Pushers are afraid of strangers, for obvious reasons. They don't usually look for new customers or need them.

Tendency to single out the pusher makes us take our eye off the ball, forget about preventive work. In sixteen drug use biographies obtained at meetings mentioned above, pushers were hardly mentioned. "My sister started me; I tried drinking, but it made me sick, so I went to marijuana," said one girl. "I started with a friend," said a young man. "I started at parties," said a Texas boy who moved to California and found pot in the sunshine. "I started in a parked car, with a group of friends," said a Jewish girl of Pennsylvania. "You finally get to where you buy it, but not at the start." "I started at college." "I met a guy; he asked me to hold his pot for him; I tried smoking it." "Kids were talking about marijuana, they said I didn't know what I was missing, so I tried it." This seamy, novelistic side of life is what we tend to forget when we reduce the drug problem to a simple matter of "A" selling a pellet to "B."

Addiction and Drug Abuse Report of May, 1970 by Grafton Publications, Inc.

Rebutting some of the "half-truths, myths, and plain lies" offered by drug proselytizers, Charles C. Dahlberg, M.D., a psychiatrist, challenges the accuracy of such oft-repeated statements as "Drugs make sex better," in *Medical Economics*, April 20, 1970. Conceding that some of the distorted perceptions caused by hallucinogenic drugs can "create at least an illusion of a more intense or prolonged sexual pleasure" he also mentioned that some patients report that under LSD, "they've gone dead in the pelvic area." It all depends on the person, the occasion, the dose, and probably other factors. In the realm of sexual pleasures, there appear to be no certainties.

His article challenges other claims: "Psychedelic drugs ease depression." There is a little truth in that one, sometimes, but not much. Even a good trip, after the spell wears off, can leave symptoms of depression.

Reacting to a statement such as, "Drugs help me understand the universe and myself," Dr. Dahlberg reminds us that some of the secrets of the universe unveiled by drugs turn out to be undecipherable and incommunicable to the voyager when he returns from the land of hallucinations.

He answers the "Drugs help me feel close to people" argument, that "feeling" is not the same as "being" and cites the reports of observers at drug parties. The users insisted they felt close to others at the parties, but in actuality they were observed to be "doing their own thing" in distinctly solitary ways. This kind of behavior is reminiscent of the all too familiar cocktail party at which the guests become convinced of their own charming humor and scintillating conversation, though nondrinkers present may find them boorish and dulled by alcohol.

Contrary to loose talk among the anti-drug forces, Dr. Dahlberg has found that addiction resulting from the first shot of heroin is by no means inevitable, and "withdrawal from heroin is (not) necessarily an agonizing experience." Nor does he find evidence complete or clearcut to substantiate the charge that "LSD will wreck your chromosomes." Many substances appear to be related to chromosome breaks. Investigators are still trying to find out what LSD is all about, and some of them think it may have potential as a psychotherapeutic adjunct when carefully used.

Other advice about loose talk comes from Professor Helen Nowlis, who cautions against classifying drugs and drug effects without reference to individual consumers and the time and place of their consumption.

". . . In the interest of good communication, let us check some of our excess baggage and not talk about "good drugs" and "bad drugs," "safe drugs" and "dangerous drugs," even "drug effects." It would be difficult to find a single drug which is not potentially dangerous for some people, under some circumstances, at some dose level. A reaction to any drug is basically the result of the interaction between an ingested or injected chemical and a physically and psychologically complex individual. It is a function of dose, of pattern and length of use of the drug, of the physiological and psychological condition of the individual, of the situation or circumstances under which it is taken, of who administers it, of the expectations of the person who administers it as well as of the person who takes it. In some instances, with the proper circumstance and expectations, placebos—normal saline solutions, sugar or lactose pills—may relieve post-operative pain, produce hallucinations, do most anything that a drug might do.

"One other fact that we should note here is what is generally referred to as "side effects." Virtually every drug has other effects, sometimes harmless, sometimes annoying, sometimes harmful."

From *"Communicating About Drugs,"* by Helen H. Nowlis, Ph.D., Professor of Psychology, University of Rochester. NIMH *Resource Book for Drug Abuse Education.* (Remarks made at National Association of Student Personnel Administrators Drug Education Conference, Washington, D.C., Nov., 1966.)

Approaches To Drug Education

Even when accurate information is presented, it has to appear relevant to the students' own idea of themselves and their personal experience. Irving L. Janis and Seymour Feshback reported on one of their experiments in dental health education, "Effects of Fear-arousing Communications," in which they found that showing pictures of horribly diseased teeth to students was less effective than a strictly neutral approach: the stimuli were apparently not consistent with their self-image, and so they dismissed them as incredible.

The severely punitive approach to problems of drug abuse followed for the past few years has obviously not prevented the increased use of marijuana, LSD, and other drugs. The rigorous laws have separated the drug-using patient from the therapist and from dependable sources of information. Distrust of enforcement agencies and of most general (if emotionally based) public attitudes drives the young user to the drug-using subculture for information.

If information from an established source is inaccurate for one drug known to young persons, they will subsequently reject more accurate data about another drug. Again, marijuana is the drug of central importance because, if our information about it is judged to be palpably inaccurate, our warnings about LSD, methamphetamine, and others, are also rejected. Self-experimentation with drugs is thereby encouraged since it is judged to be the only dependable source of information.

Frederick M. Meyers, M.D., and David E. Smith, M.D., Drug Abuse Papers, 1969. (Syllabus for Continuing Education in Criminology, University Extension, University of California, Berkeley.)

During the course of hearings before the U.S. Senate Special Subcommittee on Alcoholism and Narcotics, 1969, Senator Harold Hughes directed a question to Dr. Roger Smith, Department of Pharmacology, University of California Medical Center, San Francisco. The question related to the whole problem of drug education. Dr. Smith's reply is instructive primarily for the way *not* to approach drug education:

". . . I have been involved in a lot of drug education programs in public schools and I currently teach a course at the University of California extension primarily for teachers to handle this problem. The first thing that strikes me is that most teachers are totally ignorant of drug effects and students are able to get away with all sorts of things. When they ask them about drugs and ask them serious questions about drugs, very few teachers know how to respond. I don't know what would be the most effective approach. I have seen a number. The most common approach in the past has been to bring in a panel—usually a sociologist, a doctor, and a narcotics detective and each presents his point of view which is totally confusing to everyone and it usually ends up with a debate between the sociologist and the policeman, an experience that I have had many times. I think that is very ineffective. I think the crash programs

are very ineffective. Also, when . . . the local school board begins a weeklong program of seminars then flood the school with all sorts of pamphlets and then movies and so on. I don't think that is very effective either. . . ."

Dr. Smith is not alone in knowing how *not* to approach drug education.

. . . Untruths, exaggeration, sensationalism, and moralizing kill the effectiveness of drug education. If 20 percent of the students in a classroom of 50 have used a drug, there are at least 10 students carefully measuring the teacher's words against empirical knowledge. At least 30 students will know the 10 as users and be briefed by them. With 40 of the audience of 50 in good position to judge the accuracy of a teacher's statements about a drug he probably has never tried, any discrepancies will be quickly noted and used to breed distrust of the total presentation. . . .

An "all school" program is no way to conduct drug education. The normal rules of school are suspended, all classes stop, students assemble, people are invited from the community, and one or two films—often sensenational or lurid and more likely to breed drug use than suppress it—are shown. This "why it's dangerous to use drugs" approach is likely to make many teenagers feel that if they haven't tried drugs they're missing something.

Young people delight in pointing out the inconsistencies and hypocrisies in drug legislation and enforcement, and while they should be informed of the penalties of drug possession and use, nothing is to be gained from trying to defend the inconsistencies of drug legislation.

"How To Plan a Drug Abuse Education Workshop for Teachers," Public Health Service Publication No. 1962. (1969).

The school teacher and administrator are constantly faced with the demand to 'do something' about drug use in the school. The most common response is to invite so-called experts to lecture students on the evils of drugs. The experts are usually representatives from the local narcotic bureau or the district attorney's office. Too often they are not experts at all, and any youngster who has kept his eyes and ears open is well aware that the facts he is being presented are confounded with many lies and mistakes. Consequently he becomes suspicious and tends to reject everything the experts say.

Deterrence by fear does not work, especially when it is plainly based on ignorance. To the extent that drug usage is motivated by rebelliousness, which should, after all, be the privilege of youth, prohibition and persecution will only increase it. It is commonplace that the surest way to increase sales of an obscene book is to condemn it.

We must respect the intelligence of the young and attempt to give them an unbiased, factual picture of drug use, including the socio-legal consequences. In this way the youngster is able to weigh in his own mind the supposed pleasures of marijuana against the Draconian legal consequences. Current methods of punishment and repression will not work and will only increase the alienation and the communication gap between young and old.

Ralph Metzner, Staff Psychologist, Mendocino State Hospital. Excerpted from *"Who Needs Drug Education: Parents or Children?"* (Hearings before the U.S. Senate Special Subcommittee on Alcoholism and Narcotics, Sept., 1969.)

Whatever view you may have about what do to with or to the drug addict and drug abuser, most likely you are a good target for individuals and groups who are selling solutions to this problem.

Not only is there money to be made from the illicit importation and sale of drugs but there is money to be made from attempting to solve this increasing social problem. In a sense, both the criminal world and parts of the professional world make a living from drug abuse.

At this point in time, books, magazine articles and newspaper articles are presenting information about various facets of the drug problem. You can buy or rent films, slide kits, and other visual aid material. Kits of differing sizes containing various drugs are readily available.

Groups will sensitize you to your attitudes about drug abuse and the drug abuser. Other groups offer encounter therapy, reality therapy, behavior therapy and, of course, the more classical and conventional therapies to treat the drug abuser.

Other groups will test urine to determine if a person has used certain drugs within the last twenty-four hours. In New Jersey, during the summer of 1969, one person was offering a saliva test to determine whether a person was using various drugs. The test was fraudulent. Various communities had, however, contracted for the use of this test . . .

A drug abuse education classroom-on-wheels "licensed by a publicly held company as either Area Distributorships or Franchised Territories" is available to you. This franchise "will help communities . . . perform a great service, and also help the growth of their own business."

A drug abuse newsletter is available for you. "We believe that five minutes with one issue . . . will show up decisively in your next board meeting, your next session with a victim of drugs, your next community discussion of this problem, your next conference with a worried teacher or parent. Through the miracle of pooled and shared research, you can become the fountainhead of information in this field for your town, neighborhood and community."

You may be invited to attend a fund raising event to support a drug abuse rehabilitation program.

The services that you purchase, whether they be educational, rehabilitative or evaluative, must have meaning and relevance for the facets of the drug problem touching your community.

The people and/or groups offering these services should be checked out—what has been their track record? 1753925

Stanley Einstein, Editorial, "Be Careful: More Than Drugs Are Being Sold," from *The International Journal of the Addictions*, Dec., 1970.

Use of Ex-Addicts in Drug Programs

Often one of the first resource-people whom drug program-planners call in to "tell it like it is" is a so-called ex-addict. The technique is traditional and common. If the experience of others checks with our own observations, ex-addicts usually are eager to help but contribute little in campaigns to prevent drug abuse. Some of the reactions reported by young people reinforces our belief that ex-addicts seem to have a much more effective role in rehabilitation programs working in tandem with mental health therapists.

An articulate ex-addict gives walking, talking evidence that addiction not only can be overcome but it may even lead to a certain authority and popularity on the lecture circuit. He may give off a successful air and status that appeals to a kind of student uncertain as to his options in the "straight" world.

Other ex-addicts, according to students who have been exposed to a variety of drug education programs, have been "brainwashed," "programmed," or are "puppets" or "robots."

Opinions, however, on the effectiveness of the use of ex-addicts in drug programs vary.

Senator Harold E. Hughes, Chairman of the U.S. Senate Subcommittee on Alcoholism and Narcotics, disclosed at a seminar sponsored by the Institute for the Development of Educational Activities, that in the programs he had seen where ex-addicts and law enforcement people were used to get responses from youngsters, those young people with no drug problem seemed interested, "but they are almost totally rejected by those who are on drugs."

Use of "ex-addicts" in school programs should be approached with extreme caution. Students

often withhold credence on grounds that the ex-addict's arguments do not apply and his evidence sometimes does not stand up.

"It has been my experience," reports Commissioner Robert Dolins, Assistant Commissioner, New York State Narcotics Addiction Control Commission, "that ex-addicts have a usefulness as an image only with drug dependent individuals. Their experience and interest really does not move in the direction of the "non-user" and they tend in communities to search only for the users and experimenters. . . . (Ex-addicts) point out from their personal experience that once having become drug dependent, one can stop using drugs and become rehabilitated."

Guidelines for School Programs, The University of the State of New York, The State Education Department.

". . . We found out, however, that, with the second, third, and fourth appearance of the same addict with the same students, there was a drop in efficiency, actually a feeling of contempt, on the part of the youngsters. From this rational observation, we accepted the fact that we could efficiently use ex-addicts, as resource speakers in the classroom, once."

Joseph Langan in "Health Education Program of Los Angeles." From (Selected papers of a Seminar for Wyoming Physicians, Western Interstate Commission for Higher Education, June, 1969.)

Dr. Roger Smith in his statement before the U.S. Senate, Sept. 1969, Special Subcommittee on Alcoholism and Narcotics also said,

"I feel perhaps (ex-addicts) are less effective in educational programs, particularly in talking to high school students or grade school students in that many tend to swing to the other end of the spectrum and become very rigid and very moralistic and turn off young people almost as much as the local narcotic detectives.

". . . I think the worst approach is to use an ex-heroin addict to talk to young people about drugs that he has no knowledge of. One of the things that I think differentiates the old ghetto addict from the current addict is the fact the classical addict used heroin and stayed away from other drugs."

毒拒民國

Down with Opium and Narcotics! Anti-opium poster published by the National Anti-Opium Association of China (1928). In upper left corner is the portrait of Dr. Sun Yat-sen and his anti-opium message. The picture shows the knockout blow on the two devils; e.g., "Opium" and "morphia."

Use of Films in Drug Programs

We have heard occasional dismal reports about educational programs that ground to a halt when the wrong film was used to demonstrate the dangers of drugs. These prompt us to raise a few *caveats* about drug abuse films.

David O. Weber, film consultant to the California State Department of Public Health, suggests that drug films, like LSD can lead to some real bummers.

Audiovisual materials used in drug education programs are frequently received negatively by students. Therefore, a screening committee, with local students and parents among its members, seems advisable.

Marvin R. Levy and Sal Giarrizzo make other cautionary points on the potentials of films to carry unintended and mischievous messages.

Marvin Levy points out that it would be an obvious mistake to demonstrate how to tie a hangman's noose to a depressed individual, yet we do not think it unwise to show frustrated youngsters (assuming there are one or two in our schools) a film depicting the preparation and administration of a "fix."

Any educational attempt at relevance must begin with the realization that instruction limited to facts alone provides insufficient data upon which students can base viable decisions concerning drug abuse. Dr. Charles Winick illustrates the inadequacy of knowledge in his claim that if scientific facts alone could keep people from abusing drugs, we would not have the comparatively high level of drug abuse among physicians. Furthermore, I am continually amazed by the knowledge of drugs and the level of sophistication about drug abuse presently purported by many high school students who have become involved in the drug scene.

Marvin R. Levy, M.A., *"What Can Schools Do? A Time for Relevance."* **Paper presented to the School Health Section, American Public Health Association, 96th Annual Meeting, Detroit, Mich., Nov. 1968.**

A new cinematic genre now exists: the youth film. It began with THE GRADUATE and continued with EASY RIDER, which is even more notable because of the independence of its creators and the "personal" quality of the film. These now fashionable films follow a pattern and structure, much as the gangster, western, and war genres.

It is also very much in vogue for film critics to write long dissertations on the new genre and various species of it, sometimes praising but more often attacking them for pandering to youth, for their crass commercialism and for expressing an ideological viewpoint contrary to their own.

As film educators, it is necessary to reckon with all these phenomena since we deal directly with the instigator in all of this, i.e., the student, and in a small way must claim a place for ourselves somewhere in this labyrinth. Therefore, we must act as a safeguard against the exploitation of youth; we must help in making students aware of the possibility of ego satisfaction in anything that caters specifically to them. After all, one of our goals is to help the student arrive at a critical awareness of the medium. We must see these films and talk about them. But before we fall victim to the esoteric (as is the case with some critics), we must discuss films of this kind like any others: was it a good movie? Why? Why not? . . .

Sal Giarrizzo, "Revolution For The Sell Of It," *See* Magazine, *Film Education Issue,* September, 1970.

Conducting Surveys

In U.S. Senate Hearings before the Special Subcommittee on Alcoholism and Narcotics (Sept. 1969), Sanford Feinglass, cited that "There is considerable danger in conducting surveys at schools to find out what drugs are being used and by how many people. Foremost, the majority of students will lie to questionnaires in such surveys, partly because of suspicion of the surveyor's motives. They [students] have often seen the results of such questionnaires used in sensational exposures of which they want no part."

Attempts to survey abuse of drugs by students are often perceived by students as objects of humor and scorn.

A New York City high school teacher was determined to conduct a survey of drug-taking in her school, and gave the 11th grade health education class the task of developing a questionnaire, assisting them in the techniques of framing questions so that fraudulent answers could be detected. The students were further given the task of administering the questionnaire in classrooms.

The students undertook the survey in a spirit of earnest scientific inquiry; they built in guarantees of anonymity, assured the student body that the results of the survey would not be released to parents or the public, and that the sole reason for the survey was to determine the extent of drug experimentation, so that the curriculum could be adjusted to the realities of the students' lives. The same students were entrusted to report back to the classrooms and interpret the results of the survey.

Despite the students' pledge when they were surveyed that they would tell the truth, when the results were read back to them, shouts of "it's not true!" rang out. The students who interpreted the results to their peers gained new insight: the students who used drugs themselves tended to believe that "everybody else did," and the students who were nonusers tended to estimate a lower degree of drug use in school. Thus, they felt their survey was not so far off after all, and that drug use in the school was not as pervasive as the higher estimates of users would suggest.

Figures cited by professionals, however, are not necessarily any more accurate than the survey just described.

Professionals in the addiction field often seem addicted to playing a variation of the old numbers game. They don't place a bet with the local bookie; they publish their bets. Here are some of them:

One out of seven college students is or has been involved with some type of drug.

There are 30,000 addicts in New York City and 150,000 in the nation.

Seven percent of addicts treated in a hospital did not return to drug use for one year.

Two to three percent of the general population are alcoholics.

There are 5,000,000 alcoholics in the United States.

It's quite a widespread game. Just skim through a book, or even an article, written about alcoholism or drug addiction and you'll probably find a number.

. . . For drug addicts, the numbers come from the following sources: arrests for drug related charges (i.e., possession of drugs and/or paraphernalia needed to use drugs), voluntary commitment to rehabilitation programs, and sentencing to rehabilitation programs. These three sources in no way enumerate the numbers of people—young and old—who either occasionally misuse drugs or are addicted to them. We know that drug use has spread to suburbia. We recognize that addiction is not a monopoly of the non-whites or impoverished groups.

We also know that many individuals from certain segments of our society, although they are drug-oriented, are not arrested, jailed or committed for treatment. We know that the tensions of many jobs lead to the overuse of a variety of pills. We know that there is extremely widespread dieting with addicting drugs. None of these users is on the numbers roster.

For alcoholics, the numbers come from: arrests for alcohol-related charges (i.e., drunken driving, vehicular homicide, disturbing the peace, assault, etc.), voluntary commitment to rehabilitation and drying out programs, and court commitment to psychiatric hospitals. Once again the numbers camouflage the extent of the problem. The "Venetian blind" alcoholic, drinking alone in her apartment; the successful executive completing business deals at three-hour meals with four to six drinks; and the patient on the VIP floor, hospitalized—the records state—for a stomach condition; none of these is counted among the 5,000,000.

The misuse of drugs and alcohol affects too many of us: those we care about and those we are responsible to and for. Since one set of numbers all too often is the deciding factor in spending another series of numbers, we have the obligation to question both kinds. . . .

Stanley Einstein, Editorial "The Numbers Game," from *The International Journal of the Addictions*, Spring, 1968.

The Marijuana Market

Another favorite numbers game among drug experts, usually those who are spokesmen for law enforcement agencies, is the value of a drug haul as an index of police-efficiency. Erich Goode, Assistant Professor of Sociology, State University of New York, Stony Brook, made a nine-month study of the marijuana market, with the assistance of a grant from the National Institute of Mental Health. His findings appeared in the *Columbia Forum*, Winter, 1969, and in a British publication, *New Society*, June 11, 1970. Mr. Goode's article, "The Marijuana Market," is an example of the kind of reporting that is needed from many other areas of the drug scene:

There has been a massive increase in the use of marijuana in the United States in the past few years. Although it is impossible to state exactly how much more is consumed now than even two or three years ago, a Gallup poll conducted in the spring of 1969 indicated that almost one quarter of the American college population had tried marijuana at least once. (A similar Gallup poll taken in 1967 showed the figure to be 6 or 7 per cent.) To fill this demand, tons of marijuana move about the United States in a fairly orderly fashion. It is grown, imported, distributed and consumed according to a pattern. But how is marijuana distributed? By whom? And why?

The drug's opponents—i.e., mainly the police—claim that it is bought and sold for profit by professional criminals. Marijuana's advocates contend that, on the contrary, selling "pot," and especially giving it away, is an act of love, representing a desire to turn on the whole world to beauty and euphoria. They deny that large-scale professional dealers play a major role in marijuana distribution, for the simple reason that it is too bulky, the margin of profit too narrow, and that it can be grown, bought and distributed by too many diverse sources to interest an avaricious dealer. If anyone wished to make a sizeable profit out of selling drugs, he would handle almost any drug but marijuana. Therefore, they conclude, marijuana is distributed from top to bottom by amateurs. . . .

To get behind these discrepant views, I made a nine-month study of how marijuana is marketed. With the help of a grant from the National Institute of Mental Health, I conducted formal interviews with 204 New York City marijuana users of varied ages and backgrounds. I also questioned several marijuana dealers, receiving from them lengthy written statements describing their operations. And although my sample was not "representative," whatever that could mean in the prevailing legal climate, the information gleaned offers at least a partial glimpse into the world of marijuana distribution.

According to my informants, a reasonable price for a ton of marijuana, bought from a farmer or middleman in Mexico, is between $10,000 and $20,000, which means that it costs from $5 to $10 a pound, or less than 50 cents an ounce. A typical wholesale price in New York, buying in a bulk lot of several kilograms, is about $120 per kilo, or

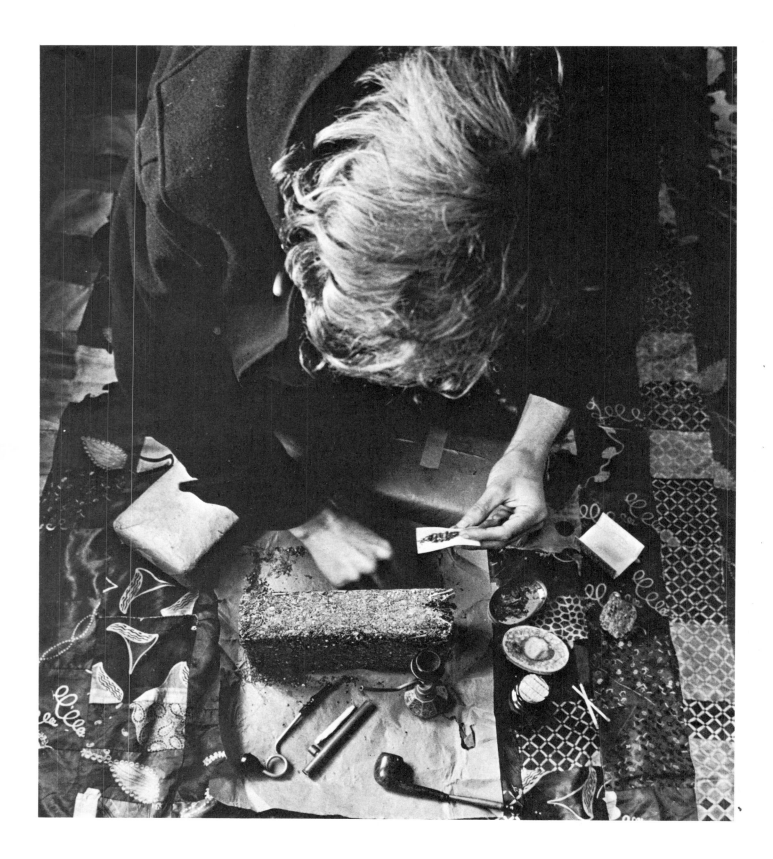

about $3.50 per ounce. (California prices are usually about half those of New York.) The retail, street, price per ounce is from $20 to $25. If a smoker wishes to purchase "joints"—individual marijuana cigarettes already rolled—he may pay between 50 cents and one dollar apiece. Thus, the markup from field to joint can be much more than 100 times—that is, buying at two joints per penny at wholesale (the ton price) and selling at one dollar a joint retail (the joint price). An enterprising dealer might thereby see in marijuana sales a source of enormous profits, but he would be making the same mistake about the workings of the marijuana market as do the police.

The joint price, one dollar, is a ghostly abstraction: today almost no one buys individual, pre-rolled joints. Nearly every smoker beyond the rawest novice rolls his own (except, I am told, in Vietnam, where large joints of excellent quality may be purchased in emptied American cigarette packs). Even when he buys the smallest "bulk" quantity, the "nickle bag," for $5, he must strain out the twigs and seeds, buy cigarette papers (the same as for tobacco roll-your-owns), and learn how to make a smokable joint. The nickle bag is a common quantity for a moderate smoker only partly caught up in the drug's subculture. In New York, the nickle bag contains between one eighth and one fourth of an ounce, enough marijuana to make between eight and 12 cigarettes, depending on the size of the joints, the dealer's generosity, and the purchaser's willingness to be shortchanged.

As the marijuana market and subculture have expanded, purchases have become much larger in bulk. . . .

If a given bulk quantity of marijuana is sitting in a dealer's living room or garage it is automatically "worth" less than if it is split up and distributed among his customers. Selling marijuana, at least at the dealer-to-user level, is hard work; each deal involves a certain amount of moving about, and a great deal of socializing. Thus, a dealer's cache of several kilograms is "worth" the wholesale price—in New York, about $120 per kilo. If sold to the customer, the cache might eventually earn $20 per ounce, but the point is, it hasn't been sold to the customer, and it is, therefore, worth correspondingly less.

Furthermore, the multi-kilo purchaser rarely earns $20 per ounce, because he doesn't generally sell in ounces. At that level, which is two or three rungs below the original source, he is most apt to break up what he has into pounds, and sell them for $100 or $120 each. He usually does not want to be bothered by ounce purchases, except as a favor to friends, because they involve too many discreet transactions; even though the margin of profit is higher if he buys several kilos and sells one or two hundred ounces, the profit on each sale is much smaller, and each transaction represents work, time—and danger. On an hour-for-hour, dollar-for-dollar basis, he comes out ahead by selling in pounds. He leaves the ounce sales to the man below him, who has bought his pound.

Yet, even this qualification simplifies the actual situation. Unlike legally sold products, a huge percentage of the marijuana that finally reaches the user is not sold at the "retail" or consumer level. A kilogram may be cut into at many different levels. Since all (or nearly all) sellers smoke, a certain portion is diverted for the dealer's own use, for which he pays wholesale prices, but on which he makes no profit. Depending on how much he smokes, he may keep perhaps half a pound out of a kilogram for his own private use. Another chunk may be given or sold at cost to close friends, offered to guests, girl friends, or used to cancel debts (as a kind of tribal barter currency). Wider out from the center (the dealer) are less intimate friends and acquaintances who might pay less than the standard prices—in New York, probably $10 per ounce. Still further out are transactions with near-strangers who are charged the full retail price. Obviously, therefore, the "leakage" from the wholesale to the retail price is considerable. . . .

The police say that the real target of their efforts is the dealer, not the user. They evidently believe that in the world of marijuana use, like that of heroin addiction, the drug peddler makes a profit from human degradation and misery, that there is a clear-cut distinction between user and seller. But in the marijuana market, the distinction is so blurred as to be meaningless.

Among my informants, nearly half (44 per cent) said that they had sold at least once. Moreover, there was a continuum from the users who had sold only once (12 per cent of those who admitted ever selling) to those who sold frequently (18 per cent of all sellers), with every shade of variation in between. One is struck by the evenness of the range of selling. In contrast to the classic pattern of pushing where there are very few sellers, nearly all of whom sell often and in gigantic quantities, many marijuana smokers sell, and characteristically do so in very small quantities. The typical seller sold a median of eight times in an average quantity of two ounces.

Far more important than the mere incidence of selling, however, is the systematic variation in selling according to certain key variables. The most important variable is how much a smoker uses: the more he smokes, the greater the likelihood that he has sold. Continued heavy use implies and even demands selling. A contrast with heroin addicts is instructive: the junkie usually consumes all that he purchases within an hour, and nearly always within 24 hours. He almost never has a "supply" of heroin, although many will save a "wake up" against withdrawal in the morning. The heavy marijuana user, on the other hand, keeps a supply, as do many occasional smokers. The more one smokes, the greater the likelihood that one will have a supply. Not one of the 26 daily smokers in my survey said that he did not have a supply of marijuana.

As a rule, even heavy marijuana smokers are not able to use up, within a brief space of time, the quantities they purchase. Often a sale is on a "take it or leave it" basis. A quantity available might be an ounce, in which case none of it is sold, or a pound or a kilogram, in which case most of it is sold. Even the daily marijuana smoker is not so committed to his drug of choice that he would be willing to tolerate a daily, twice-daily, thrice-daily, routine of obtaining small quantities of quickly used-up marijuana. That would be considered a needless "hassle." The only way to limit his transactions, and thus his exposure to arrest, is to purchase large amounts. By buying a pound at the near-wholesale price of $120, and selling 12 ounces to 12 friends for $10 an ounce, he has four ounces free. Thus "free grass" is an inducement for selling.

On the surface, there is a close parallel with the heroin addict: each sells to "support the habit," and gets nothing else out of it. Yet, even if the marijuana seller smoked 10 joints a day, an enormous quantity (not one of my 204 respondents smoked that much), he would consume a pound every three or four months, which means that his "habit" would cost one dollar a day, at the most. If he smoked a much more common two joints a day,

his "habit" would cost him about 20 cents a day at the near-wholesale price, 50 to 75 cents a day at the retail, one-ounce price, and nothing if he did some judicious selling. We should discard the "support the habit" explanation for selling, therefore, and look instead to the web of social relations in which the user-seller is implicated for some clue to his dealing habits.

Every marijuana user invariably has friends who also use marijuana. Indeed, there is a direct correlation between the amount a person smokes and the percentage of his friends who smoke and a high probability that they will buy and sell from each other. Moreover, because of his friendships, a regular smoker is more likely than a novice to have access to information about the periodic availability of marijuana on the market, to know others who buy and sell, and who are higher up in the distribution ladder. He is more acquainted with the price system, which fluctuates even in the short run. He knows more about the necessary precautions to avoid arrest, about thefts, "burns," and being short-changed, and about how to avoid adulterated goods. He can buy and sell successfully and with confidence. Anyone arriving on the marijuana scene as a complete stranger would encounter difficulty in making a large purchase.

There is, then, a two-way process at work here. First, one must be implicated in a web of social relations in order to be able to purchase the drug. But friendship is also an active force in insuring one's involvement in selling. In addition, by buying and selling, a smoker extends his network of acquaintances, almost all of whom are marijuana users. In short, friendships and sales interact with one another; they are inseparable elements of a single dimension; their relationship with one another must be seen in dialectical terms, rather than as simple cause and effect. . . .

. . . A large percentage of users sell, and nearly all sellers use. Indeed, the determining force behind selling is use: heavy users are very likely to sell; infrequent users are unlikely to do so. Selling marijuana, then, to some degree presupposes involvement with the marijuana subculture; in fact, selling is a surer indicator of involvement in the drug subculture than is buying or using, although it also implies at least a moderate degree of use. To think of the dealer as "preying" on his helpless victim, the marijuana smoker, and as profiting from his misery, is to possess a ludicrous and grotesquely incorrect view of the real state of affairs. In large part, the seller is the user, and if any preying is being done, he is preying on himself. . . .

What of the organized professional criminal? Has my portrait eliminated him altogether? Yes—and no. The largest recent seizure of marijuana from Mexico was about a ton. An operation of that size obviously requires a certain degree of organization. A microbus has to be specially outfitted for the job, middlemen in Mexico negotiated with, drivers hired, at least a dozen high-level dealers contacted for distribution. It is not Cosa Nostra style organization, but it is organization. If we mean by "organized crime," a tightly knit, nation-wide syndicate involving thousands of committed gangsters, whose entire livelihood derives from illegal activities, then marijuana is not sold, never has been sold, and probably never will be sold by professional criminals. If, however, we mean a semi-independent operation involving a score of individuals whose activities are coordinated, and who earn their living for a few years from marijuana sales, then it is true that marijuana is often sold by professional criminals. Just how much of the total of marijuana consumed derives from this kind of source is impossible to determine: in bulk, it may be a majority.

That is why a consideration of the level at which a deal takes place is so important. The importer is often a criminal: his livelihood is importing marijuana; he is a capitalist who sells an illegal product. But he has no particular commitment to marijuana as an agent of mind-transformation, an element in a subculture, or a catalyst in social change. He probably does not even smoke marijuana. The unsystematic practices of "head" dealers created a vacuum into which he stepped. The multi-kilogram, top-level dealers to whom the importer sells are also primarily profit-seekers but—and this is the crucial difference—they deal with consumers as well as other dealers, and are very likely to be consumers themselves. As the marijuana continues to be divided and sold in smaller quantities, the profit motive of the seller becomes less dominant. At the link next to the consumer, friendship transactions are extremely common. Thus, to say that marijuana is a business is both true and false. At some levels it is; at others, it is not. To say that it is big business is misleading. A monthly take of a quarter of a million dollars, split 20 ways, might represent the very top of the profession. A bit lower down, even a dedicated hustler earns what an unskilled factory worker might make. Below that, the profit motive breaks down entirely.

A common argument against marijuana smoking is that it leads to association with criminals, to trying heroin, to committing serious crimes. But the average American user never comes into contact with the underworld, even if every gram he smokes comes ultimately from a tightly organized network of full-time professional gangsters. The typical marijuana smoker has no idea where his marijuana comes from. It has been filtered down through so many levels and has exchanged hands so many times, that the average user is no more likely to come in contact with a top-level seller than would a cigarette smoker with a tobacco auctioneer or a Wall Street lawyer with a Hong Kong tailor. The chain is long, and the links are many. Each step downward involves a change in character of the personnel. In short, the average user buys his marijuana from a friend—even though it probably derived, originally, from a gangster.

Thus, the argument that the penalties for marijuana possession and use should be reduced, but that they should be retained for selling, violates empirical reality; it implies the existence of two relatively distinct social and moral spheres. In fact, if the seller is guilty, the user is too, because the user is often the seller, and the seller the user. The technical exchange of contraband goods for money takes place at every conceivable level and by nearly everyone above the minimally involved. Labelling all selling heinous, and use only moderately reprehensible, is to display ignorance of the workings of the market. . . .

Erich Goode in "The Marijuana Market," from *New Society*, June 11, 1970. Originally in *Columbia Forum*, Winter, 1969.

In the next chapter, selections deal with more specific ideas that can be tried in the area of drug abuse prevention. Many of these ideas are taken from the wisdom of experienced practitioners. The fact that everybody is learning a lot about drugs so quickly suggests that we can learn better ways to prevent drug abuse. As Kenneth Boulding put it, "Once you've wised up, you can't wise down."

Chapter Four

THINGS TO KNOW AND DO

During the preparation of this book, our (the editors') convictions were strengthened that knowledge, per se, will not prevent drug abuse, and that looking toward clear, mechanistic solutions usually leads to mistaken hopes and broken expectations. We are hopeful that there will be new discoveries in many directions to help people learn how to put their own life to optimal use, so that drugs will seem superfluous. We may yet learn to tap the secrets locked in our own bodies, to control our own nervous systems so that stresses, pains and pleasures can be self-directed. Until that time has come, the best we can hope is that man will come to terms with the idea that turning to drugs is turning away from life, and from the obligation we all have to find life's meaning. The insights gathered in this chapter are concerned with living a good life unto death. Despair and false hopes in this connection seem to turn people toward drugs.

In choosing selections for this chapter, we found it useful to compile a list of "articles of faith" which we have come to share. Perhaps this list will be beneficial to other collaborators. Some of our articles of faith may have appeared in other chapters, but here they seem especially pertinent to the ancient process of living a good life.

Help comes from the most unlikely places. Ask first what makes you feel better than your favorite indulgences. Look to the body, the senses, the imagination, the memory, the yearnings of spirit, the needs of the psyche, and ask what *they* want that this cigarette, this beer, this chocolate bar, this cup, this vapor, this pill, this needle will not satisfy.

Help comes from institutions that have long sought to satisfy these needs: family, friends, dance, sport, exercise, calisthenics, sleep, relaxation, silence, music, sensual stimulants, perceptions, nature, poetry, religion, food, drama, literature, useful work, games, politics, people in need, walking, talking, sharing. Look to all places where people strive for excellence, for precision, for control, for esthetics, for release, and for integration.

Help remake these organizations and institutions. Push them as John Gardner says. Join and insist that they respond to each other, reinforce each other, and flourish in the environments where they are most desperately needed, where the greatest damage has been inflicted upon people.

Keep an open mind about what the individual personality may need; encourage each person to explore his uniqueness, to strengthen the self that offers promise of individuality and liberation, the self that society needs, but may not recognize until it has been actualized.

Keep options open for life. Be ready for new ideas and actions. In dealing with problems, learn to scan one's options quickly, also to weigh them carefully, and to search for new ones. At all times recognize that one's situation is never limited to two alternatives, but instead that many options wait to be discovered.

Invest in the celebration of life by investing in the environment that sustains life systems in balance.

Know the structuring principles that build living cells, organs, individuals, groups, and communities; understand the entropic process by which elements in the universe tend to "run down" into disorganization, chaos, death. Restructure that which must be restructured in the interests of life and growth.

Death is a viable alternative only when all other options have been exhausted, and the player is ready to commit his energy to the mystery from which it came, with terror neither for darkness nor light.

⎸ Youth, Where It All Begins

L. M. Schulman, in his foreword to *The Loners: Short Stories About the Young and Alienated,* speaks of youth as the time when we must discover a number of things—always alone—never alone:

We are always alone. We are never alone. Even in the center of a crowd of friends, we cannot escape our apartness; even in a locked and darkened room, we cannot cut ourselves off from our sense of the life going on outside.

There are exceptions: moments of love and mystical union, or flights into the perfect solitude of madness. But for the most part, we make our peace with the paradox. We cover over the contradiction in our lives with layers of indifference. There it remains, unseen, unfelt, unhealing.

The young, however, have no such protection. Youth may well be a time of wonder and joy. What is more certain is that it is a time of disillusionment, anger, rebellion and loneliness. For this is when we must discover who we are, what the world is, and the elusive nature of our relationship to it.

L. M. Schulman in *The Loners: Short Stories About the Young and Alienated.*

William L. Lynch in *Christ and Apollo,* states that "There are two basically contrary and hostile positions now held by the contemporary imagination regarding time . . .

"According to one, time is a thing that must be escaped from, since it leads neither to insight, beauty, God, peace nor to anything else. It must either be destroyed or immobilized—or must be used in such a manner as clearly indicates that it is external to ourselves. . . .

"The other position: nothing but ourselves, as we move without pause through all the phases and stages of our lives."

Our youth do not appear to be looking for eternity, except possibly through looking inward to the eternal nature of an existentialist now. For them there is often eternity enough in the time on hand. Perhaps some young people find time so insupportable that they seek to destroy and immobilize it, as in Lynch's phrase. And drugs can kill time, or make it unrecognizable.

Ecclesiastes' insistence that there is nothing new under the sun was an attempt to de-emphasize time and set men free from their timebound condition.

Life has certain lessons that one must learn at some time or other, and a sizeable number of them fall upon youth. Dr. Lewis Judd of the Department of Psychiatry of the University of California School of

Medicine observes that adolescence is a time of life marked by emotional turbulence and turmoil, which creates problems for the adolescent, his family, and society in general. The psychological development that occurs at this time can be organized into developmental tasks, which emphasize the purposefulness of adolescence. To understand today's teen-agers there should be an understanding of the process and purpose of adolescence itself.

For normal psychological development, Dr. Judd has outlined the nine tasks confronting the adolescent (during approximately 10 years, from ages 11 to 21). The selection does not attempt to instruct the young in ways to master the developmental process for coming of age:

1. *The establishment of independence from parents and other adults.* During normal adolescence there is resistance to the influence and opinions of parents. The adolescent becomes more skeptical, more argumentative, opinionated, and negativistic. He is a notoriously poor listener. There is friction in the family, with quarrels over the use of the car, dating, smoking, drinking, choice of friends, homework, the spending of money, education, and vocational plans.

2. *The arrival at a stable self-concept or self-definition.* The establishment of a stable identity is probably one of the more basic tasks of adolescence. The adolescent comes to recognize his capabilities and weaknesses and he is apt to experiment with a multitude of roles and choices verbally, in action, and in fantasy. Young people cannot be expected to know automatically what kind of persons they want to be as adults. Adolescence is a time of experimentation from day to day, but the overall purpose is serious and the end results relatively permanent.

3. *The development of self-motivation and self-determination.* It is necessary for the adolescent to be able to rely on himself as a primary source for personal initiative and direction. Young people during adolescence begin to show increasing resistance and reluctance to act when adults try to oversee or direct their behavior. There is

a continual need for more responsibility along with recognition of the growing self-reliance.

4. *The establishment of an appropriate set of values.* By establishing an appropriate set of values the adolescent acquires the concepts and rules of conduct that are necessary for living in a society as an adult. During adolescence there is apt to be a passionate attachment to causes, to philosophical principles and ideas, and a readiness to discuss them at length. Commitment to, or skepticism toward, religion is likely to occur between the ages of 14 and 16 and the rules of society frequently come under question.

5. *The development of understanding and sympathy for others and of reciprocity in interpersonal relationships.* The ability to feel tenderness, respect, and concern for others is a major step in emotional development. It involves being able to achieve one's own goals without trampling on the rights of others, and understanding of the reasons for the actions of other people.

6. *The establishment of an appropriate sexual identity and the development of wholesome relationships with members of the opposite sex.* Physical changes during puberty are fairly rapid and often the teen-ager is not prepared to understand or adjust to these rapid changes. The unreadiness of adolescents is often expressed through their unhappiness with their own physical characteristics. There is always something they obsessively wish could be changed, such as their complexion, weight, height, body proportions, facial features, teeth—almost anything. Preoccupation with physical appearance is a compelling force. As puberty advances sexual drives become more urgent. Outlets are masturbation (admitted by 88 percent of males and 40 percent of the females); fleeting sexual experiences during early adolescence with members of the same sex (admitted by 27 percent of the males and 15 percent of the females); and sexual activities with members of the opposite sex, including petting and sexual intercourse. As adolescence progresses the need for adjustment to the opposite sex increases in importance and a proper sexual role is solidified by accepting

oneself as a sexually mature person who can both control and enjoy sexual feelings.

7. *The development of new intellectual capacities and skills.* Much research has been given to emotional and physical changes during adolescence, but little documentation has been provided for changes in intellectual functions. Abstract thinking, perspectives of past and future, and intellectual functioning are apt to be very close to adult levels by the age of 16 years.

8. *The development of the ability to function satisfactorily with age mates and to behave properly with others in the peer group.* The influence of the peer group (others of the same age and development) is very strong. Most adolescents conform and nonconformists are rejected and ridiculed by the group. The adolescent group usually has its own music, style of dress, language, and values. The ability to function within this adolescent society is necessary to gain appropriate social rewards.

9. *The acquisition of training, or participation in a training program, that will develop the skills for achieving economic independence.* The development of self-reliance is an essential step on the part of the adolescent for supporting a family of his own. The completion of this task signals the end of adolescence.

Large numbers of adults leave adolescence without having achieved emotional or economic independence; thus in our society there are many adults who are still struggling with "adolescent" problems. At least a reasonable amount of achievement in each of the nine developmental tasks of the normal adolescent is necessary, for it is on this base that the psychological growth and maturity of the adult will be built.

Adults must judge adolescence by its own processes and purposes, not by adult standards.

Lewis J. Judd's article, "The Normal Psychological Development of the American Adolescent," which originally appeared in *California Medicine*, December, 1967. Abstract of the article is from Oliver E. Byrd's *Medical Readings on Drug Abuse.*

Family Matters

". . . a family lasts, for a while: the children are held to a magnetic center; then in time, the magnetism weakens, both of itself and its tiredness of aging and sorrow, and against the strength of the growth of each child, and against the strength of pulls from the outside, and one by one the children are drawn away." So James Agee observed in *Let Us Now Praise Famous Men.*

Arthur Mandelbaum as Chief Psychiatric Social Worker at the Menninger Foundation, feels that a family has contributed its share to civilization if it "gives its children a true sense of freedom and liberation within a form which is coherent and is accompanied by a sense of trust and self-esteem."

Much has been said about the need for parents to listen to their children and to talk openly and honestly with them, or the children will be left to their own resources and to the incomplete knowledge and partial wisdom of peers. But parents also have peer-groups, and perhaps some effort should be made on their part to examine their own peer-pressures. There is a good deal of advice available to parents about helping their young children develop, and somewhat less valuable advice about the continuing development of parents, that will help prepare them for gracious grandparenthood. Apparently many parents have been "doing something right" that helped their children cope with the vicissitudes of life without depending on drugs.

...What can we tell parents from our experience? First, that parents should learn as much as they can about the drugs, so they can speak intelligently, knowledgeably, and openly with their teenagers and try to take away some of the mystique, to get involved with their teenagers, to listen to them. After all, they're pretty well educated, intelligent people, with pretty refreshing ideas. The parent, above all, has to be a parent, not a pal or a buddy, because only a parent can provide the necessary discipline and involvement that parenthood requires. Lastly, we plead with parents. Don't give up! Even if your child does get picked up by the police. Don't give up on him. This may be the time he needs you most.

Ira Frank, M.D., in *Psychedelic Drug Abuse Among Our Youth* (Seminar for Wyoming Physicians, Western Interstate Commission for Higher Education, June, 1969).

Parents need to reassess their own attitudes and use of drugs. They need to reassert their dominance in providing activities and recreation for their children, not only in early childhood but later as well. Young children need reassurance in their abilities to set limits. As Richard H. Blum of Stanford has said, special agencies can assist in providing recreational outlets, but this is only ancillary and not a take-over. Early in life children have to be shown ways of resisting peer pressures, which is the basic pattern of the spread of drug use later.

Open dialogue on drugs is imperative. Within the limitations of time, I have talked to ghetto boys clubs, ministerial associations, hospital auxiliaries, Senior Citizens and medical societies, but this needs to be done more widely.

Roswell D. Johnson, M.D., in "Box Seats at the Drama" from *Brown Alumni Monthly*, December 1969, Vol. 70, No. 3.

Parent Approaches to Teen and Subteen Drug Abuse

Herbert O. Brayer and Allan Y. Cohen give further advice to parents concerning drug abuse prevention.

1. Have frank, open and frequent family discussions about drug use and abuse.
2. Adopt a sincere attitude of being a student yourself as far as drug matters are concerned:

   a. Be a student of drug use literature and educational materials.

   b. Be a student of your children regarding the local drug scene; they'll know more about it than most so-called authorities.

   c. Study challenging and zestful alternatives to drug abuse through discussion with your children; find alternatives that *they are interested in;* get reliable information not biased or propagandistic.

3. Don't "buy" propaganda and avoid moralizing and "preaching"—both turn students "off" and have little real effect.

4. Project confidence in your child or teen-ager's

ability to make decisions. Teach them from facts how to make generalizations, to form attitudes, and from these to see personal and lasting values. Then teach them to use their knowledge and values in making decisions that only they can make for themselves.

5. *Be a parent*, not a buddy! *You* must establish the standards—the *values*—for your home. Your *legal* as well as moral responsibility lasts until your child is 21 or married! You and your spouse must set the "rules" of the game and these should be fair but firm. Insist on playing by these "rules" and don't let them fall into disuse. Your children must know what you expect of them—play, study, hours, clothing, deportment, manners, etc. So you will be a "square" to them . . . so what? That's better than being parents of a "head" or dope user (or worse)!

   a. Know where your child is at all times and whom they are with.
   b. Avoid *all* unchaperoned parties (beach, theater, mountains, slumber, etc.) for *all* your *underage* children.
   c. Plan *family* affairs regularly and for your children (picnics, parties, outings, shows, athletic events, church, fishing, hunting, shopping, and theaters). Your grandmother used to say, "Idle hands are the devil's workshop." You'd better believe it, but remember to obtain and maintain family identity on an "activity basis." Avoid "boredom" and "there's nothing to do on this island."
   d. Plan and demand "responsibility." Children can't mature as *responsible* persons unless *given responsibility*. Every child should have things for which he/she is responsible. The old but valued concept of "chores" or "duties" *is* character building. Authorities tell us these should start as early as possible—long before Kindergarten. Remember, a child can't be responsible unless he knows responsibility (lawns, garden, room, dishes, yard, laundry or clothes, car cleaning or washing, etc., etc.). These must be on a *daily basis*, not occasionally. Mother and Dad *must see* that these are really done.
   e. Be prepared for "I don't want to do it," or "I don't want to go with you Sunday," etc. As a parent *you are* the "boss." You must

make being a parent work. (Again, it's better than being the mother of a drug-head, isn't it?) Resistance will go down proportionally as you insist on *your way* and as you explain your views and diversify your program. But it is too late to start this after your child has reached adolescence! Start as early in your boy's or girl's life as possible—long before Kindergarten.

6. Realize your importance as a model for your children! They want Dad as a "model" and Mother *is* their "model" despite other circumstances.

7. Give active personal support and offer real cooperation to community and school innovative drug abuse programs and projects. *Get involved!*

8. Avoid arguing with your children about legalization or the legitimacy of drug laws. Emphasize instead the personal effects, long and short term, of drugs on them personally and then on other human beings. *Don't get trapped in an argument!*

9. Separate the issue of drugs from the problems of the so-called "generation gap." Don't be trapped into relating these separate problems; it's like comparing apples and bananas.

10. Be prepared to work on your own problems of drug use and misuse. Remember the proven facts concerning the drugs in tobacco, liquor, etc., that you may ingest regularly and which your children have learned are often worse for the human being than other drugs may prove to be. Don't excuse or hide *your* problem. Be honest with your kids or expect them to use that ugly word "hypocrite."

11. Refrain from building your guilt complex over your children's drug abuse. Every youth problem isn't necessarily the result of parent failure.

12. Recognize and understand that drug *use* generally is sanctioned and even encouraged by American Society (alcohol, nicotine, caffeine, prescribed and non-prescribed mood drugs such as tranquilizers or "downers," amphetamines or "uppers," sleeping pills, diet pills, even aspirin, etc.). *It is abuse and misuse that's the problem.*

13. When in doubt assume your child *IS* experimenting with drugs. Don't panic, climb the

wall, beat or throw your child out in the cold! Start communicating on a *"WE* have a problem basis,"* and "how can *WE* meet and solve it." Don't moralize! Your communication must be on a "man to man" basis, not on an outraged "criminal" one. Establish the rules of the game fairly and mutually. You can't run a prison successfully in your own home so redevelop "trust" and strive for communication and understanding.

14. Be prepared to refer your teen-ager or child to proper agencies for emotional guidance and counseling—to qualified people in the behavioral sciences such as psychologists, psychiatrists, physicians, social workers, school counselors, or trusted teachers.

15. As a last resort—only *AFTER* frankly explaining the reasons to the teen-ager—take him or her to the juvenile authorities and give them a complete and frank statement of your problem. Then follow their advice and don't try to "second guess" them.

16. During the next twelve months, help meet the overall problems of your children and those of your neighbors by taking an active role in forwarding the innovative educational programs planned by your local school district to meet the changing economic, political, and social scene as well as needs of our young generation. We must more and more lay our stress on children finding and fulfilling their own potentials as against the grade-orienting competition which is causing so many to either "cop out" or turn to drugs. Our schools must lay greater emphasis on teaching *attitudinal development* ("valuing"), *responsibility* and *sound decision-making*, along with the transmission of facts based on scientific research and development. Your school board, administrators, and dedicated teachers are working day and night to realize this program as quickly and effectively as resources, time, and human energies permit! *BUT*, they will fail miserably without your active concern and deliberate help on the family and community front!

Herbert O. Brayer, Coordinator, Drug Abuse Prevention Education, Orange County Department of Education, Santa Ana, California, and Allan Y. Cohen, John F. Kennedy University, Martinez, California, in "Parent Approaches To Teen and Subteen Drug Abuse."

During testimony before the U. S. Senate Special Subcommittee on Alcoholism and Narcotics, Dr. Roger Smith, University of California Medical Center, San Francisco, was asked some questions about family and social pressures.

Senator Dominick. In your opinion is family social pressure against the use of drugs helpful or harmful?

Dr. Smith. It depends on what form that pressure takes. I have known of a number of young people who have become very deeply involved in drug use and after their parents found out they were using marihuana, became so upset they told them to get out of the house and when you have decided to straighten up, and abide by our rules, then we will take you back. Of course, they can find friends in the drug scene. The drug scene is not very discriminating. They take almost anybody. So if you want to push that kind of pressure, I think it makes the problem worse. Senator Hughes described one technique that I think might be effective—that you talk over the reasons for using drugs, what do you expect to get out of it? What kind of harm do you think it will do to you or do to us? Whatever you do we are still here, we are still your parents and we will still love you and will still take you back. I think the parents, however, can make it much worse by forcing children out on to the streets and alienating them entirely.

Senator Dominick. So in general would you say that the family and social pressures which militate against the use of drugs is harmful despite the fact that drugs themselves are harmful?

Dr. Smith. I don't recall saying that. What I said is that pressures can be used—good or bad—depending on how they are exerted. If you become very self-righteous and moralistic and screaming at your child and telling him he is going to hell because he smoked a joint, then you are probably doing more harm than good. If you don't panic and if you understand that this is something that the young person has to work out, that you ought to probably get involved in it and try to help him think it out, then lend to him your concern and your desire that he not use drugs then maybe that kind of pressure is helpful.

Senator Dominic. You are coming back to the question of the use of marihuana. What about speed, should you lay any kind of pressures against using this?

Dr. Smith. Certainly. I think the same kind of pressures that you would use if you walked in on your child smoking marihuana in his bedroom. You would help him deal with his problem. I think again you would make it much worse by telling him —by throwing him out. We have seen many an example of this.

Senator Dominick. I am not talking about throwing him out. I am not talking about that type of thing. I am talking about an attitude of a family being against the use of drugs.

Dr. Smith. If you can be against the use of drugs and still not be against your son or your daughter and not close off any line of communication, then perhaps that kind of pressure can be effective.

Senator Hughes. I might add that certainly is my attitude. I am against the use of drugs. I intend to use the most intelligent way hopefully that I can to try and convince my children—two of whom are adults and one still in her teens—that there is no need for it or the use of it, and it is a bad thing.

Dr. Roger Smith, Dept. of Pharmacology, University of California Medical Center, San Francisco, testifying before the Special Subcommittee on Alcoholism and Narcotics, Committee on Labor and Public Welfare, U.S. Senate, Sept., 1969.

"Keeping the lines of communication open" ought to be easy in a family where there was adequate communication from the start. Novelists and playwrights have dealt with the problems of communication in the unhappy family before and since Oedipus Rex, and there is no dearth of dialogue to support the necessity of one human being to relate to other human beings.

Under and Over Thirty—And Trustworthy

The four selections that follow are about communicating on any level that builds trust. We think the techniques described will help all people who are trying to communicate, whether the effort is directed toward getting in touch with one's own feelings, one's friends and family, or the wider community.

As a social psychologist, I would like to talk about the dynamics of communication in any educational process. . . .

First, it is most important for communicators about drug use to have made a sincere assessment of their own goals and motivations. We may define the issues and present the best and most objective information as frankly as we can and then trust the student to make his own decision. On the other hand, if we have already decided what students should do and we feel that the risks in letting them make their own decisions are too great, we may selectively use information to explain or justify our position. Either approach is defensible and each presents its own problems, but all concerned should be aware of which position is being taken. We run into all kinds of problems if we waver from one to the other or appear to be operating under one approach when we are really operating under the other. You cannot say, as so many parents do: You decide—as long as you decide my way. In the area of the use and abuse of drugs by college students, either position presents complex problems.

Second, the communicator must have clearly thought through the issues in his own mind. It is probably wise to clearly separate the question of the dangers or abuse of individual drugs, both physical and psychological, from the question of legality. When a presentation of the untoward effects of a drug, even the potential untoward effects, is designed to support the illegal status of the drug, battle lines are drawn on the basis of individual rights vs. arbitrary authority and invasion of privacy, and none of the relevant issues is open to rational, unemotional consideration.

Third, effective communication has been shown to be a function of the prestige of, respect for and credibility of the communicator. It has been demonstrated that attempts at persuasion based on a high fear appeal are generally ineffective and may boomerang, especially with subjects of high intelligence. This type of appeal invariably casts doubt on the credibility and motivations of the communicator. An audience which becomes concerned with testing credibility will be distracted from the real issues presented in the communication.

The final factor that should be mentioned with respect to the communicator is the fact that if an audience has some knowledge about or attitudes toward an issue, all sides of an argument should be fairly presented. This does not necessarily mean that there should be dramatic confrontation between diametric opposites. It does mean that, as a minimum, the evidence for opposing views should be fairly presented. Neither does this mean that the communicator should not present his own considered view together with the reasons for it. In fact, one of the necessary functions of a teacher or an administrator is to draw conclusions, take a stand, but it should be clear that this stand is taken after careful consideration of all points of view.

. . . I hope I have left you with the impression that we have no nice package to present. In the absence of facts, there is no need to pretend that we know. We can present hypotheses, trends, hunches as long as they are labeled as such and presented as tentative, awaiting data which will support or refute them. . . .

Helen H. Nowlis, Ph.D., Professor of Psychology, Univ. of Rochester, in "Communicating About Drugs," remarks made at National Association of Student Personnel Administrators Drug Education Conference, Washington, D. C., November, 1966. NIMH *Resource Book for Drug Abuse Education.*

Knowledge is a prelude to understanding. If you work with students in the area of drugs, you must become as informed as possible. Do the basic reading: be able to cite relevant sources. . . . But also be very humble. Students will quickly reject your expertise on drugs if you over-represent your wisdom. Students are increasingly sophisticated and, if you get caught in an unfounded conclusion or a flip generalization, you might rapidly lose your effectiveness. You need not have taken drugs to be able to communicate relevant facts about their effects, as long as you are honest.

It is best to approach the psychedelic user (or potential user) without preconceived ideas. Mass media to the contrary, he is not necessarily sick, nor is he necessarily irresponsible. Approach a user as you would any other human being in the process of development. Interestingly, the kinds of students most attracted to psychedelics tend to be those whom we might consider the most dynamic, creative, and imaginative. Based on research I did at Harvard, the psychedelic user is likely to be quite different from the kind of individual who becomes dependent on narcotics, barbiturates, tranquilizers, or alcohol. Most students seem to use psychedelics not so much to *forget what they*

already have, but to *discover and attain what they have not*. I would suggest that the majority of young people experimenting with such materials be respected for their courage in exploration, for their curiosity, and for their conscious or unconscious commitment to self-discovery. Unfortunately, these basically positive instincts are usually misdirected and perverted through the use of psychedelics. . . .

There are two major accomplishments of a truly sympathetic orientation toward student drug involvement. First, it makes all further efforts more credible and effective. Secondly, an open, honest, and understanding approach to the student (or hippie) shakes up his preconceptions of you as the "square authoritarian" which you inherit because of your role as part of the Establishment. It can go a long way in melting the barriers of fear and mistrust, opening the way for fruitful dialogue.

Allan Y. Cohen, Ph.D., Associate Professor of Psychology and Director of the Institute for Drug Abuse Education and Research, John F. Kennedy University, Martinez, Calif., in "Psychedelic Drugs and the Student: Educational Strategies" (*Journal of College Student Personnel*, March, 1969.)

Need For Communication

Robert C. Petersen, Chief of the Center of Studies on Narcotic and Drug Abuse, National Institute of Mental Health, stresses the *need for teachers* and other *adults* to communicate with young people by that highly effective yet perhaps most difficult means —personal example. He draws attention also to the value of finding alternatives and of sublimating feelings of powerlessness and outrage at social injustice.

Recognize Your Role as A Model. Because teenagers seem to be engrossed in the activities of their own age group, we may forget that teachers often play a significant role as models for their development.

It may be helpful for the teacher who presently smokes or formerly smoked to freely acknowledge the difficulties he experienced in attempting to give up the habit. Emphasizing that it is not easy to alter persistent habits may be of value. Habits such as use of tobacco and alcohol can illustrate the highly persistent nature of habitual behavior despite strong rational grounds for change.

Adults can also serve to demonstrate that it is possible to live a rewarding life without the use of chemical substances to add meaning or excitement. The adult who is "turned on" by life without recourse to drugs is one of the best deterrents to drug abuse.

Encourage Interest in Alternatives to Drug Abuse. Youngsters who find satisfaction in other activities are less likely to find drugs appealing. Many young people feel keenly the problems of our contemporary world. They need to be involved in activities that have personal meaning. Such activities as working for a political party or in programs for slum children can serve as concrete contributions for coping with contemporary problems. . . .

Robert C. Petersen in "Suggestions for Educators," *N.E.A. Journal,* March, 1969.

Joseph F. Maloney, Director, Urban Studies Center, University of Louisville, Kentucky, put his finger on one irony in cross-generational communication. Although the older person should understand the younger because he has *already* been young, quite the opposite may be true. If so, it may account for a good deal of the arrogance of elders toward youth.

. . . . I suggest the young understand us better than we understand them—better than they communicate to us. They tune us in and understand our language, but we do not necessarily understand the words they use or the patterns with which they use words. More, they communicate in a style that we reject as outrageous, thoughtlessly rejecting their thoughts because they are not presented to us in our style. . . .

They are not politicians, in that they are incapable of inventing and working diligently for a new system. They reject without being able to design a well-thought substitute. They are not philosophers because they cannot synthesize a comprehensive and systematic approach to life. They certainly don't talk like the politicians we are used to, and they don't produce logical arguments or rhetoric like our honored prose literature.

But they are poetical. They do have sharp insights into truth, which they do express very imaginatively and suggestively, rather than precisely. We made them poets. We subjected them to the TV, radios and other media as the message that has molded their patterns of perception and intellection. The Saturday morning TV cartoons have exposed them to more mind-expanding fairy tales— talking animals and heroes seen as such—than we were exposed to.

. . . Because we must have a commercial every six minutes or less on TV and every three minutes on the radio, they are accustomed to short, explosive communications. . . . They see fast—they have been trained that way before they get to school. They see things in extremes—the commercial is punchy, and the interval between commercials is too short to develop complicated arguments or to distinguish shades of gray.

They understand our language style—but reject it. Rhetoric is boring. Distinctions are evasions. We take too long to say little—and much of what we say is trivial.

Look at the tremendous intellectual and spiritual problems teachers must wrestle with. Ladies may wear evening pants and party pajamas to presidential inaugural balls—but they are too risque for high schools. If a faculty prohibits slacks for girls they will merely confirm the not altogether unfounded student opinion that the faculty is from another world, a world of the past—a past irrelevant to modern life. . . .

Youth will seek life. Let them find us among the living. Then—and only then—can we share life together.

Dr. Joseph F. Maloney in "Communication With Youth," an outline of a talk before a pilot workshop in Louisville. From National Institute of Mental Health *Resource Book for Drug Abuse Education,* 1969.

We do not mean that mature adults need to adopt the language and life-style of the young, an unseemly and perhaps even counterfeit line of action. In our own attempts to leap over the dread barrier between the generations, we have brought together on numerous occasions young drug-using students and their non-using peers to help us understand both groups and the pressures at work on them. We have sought answers from them as to the kind of directions and support they needed from responsible adults. We have made no attempt to use the drug cult jargon, except for the purpose of eliciting definitions and clarifications, and as a means of bringing out a better understanding of different terminologies by different people, and, hopefully, a better understanding of one another.

The young are gifted at backhand compliments. The so-called Drug Information Director in a New York City high school, after recruiting students to help him start their program, set about getting the "right kind" of teachers to join them in creating a counter culture, in that overcrowded school. The students ticked off the names of teachers they hoped would make their way down to the cubbyhole next to the boiler room that serves as "Head Office," or Drug Information Office. The students sent out an invitation for all interested teachers to come down and join in, and some twenty teachers appeared within the next few days. One volunteer teacher of mature years not known for her levity arrived and apologetically stated that she wanted to "do something" but she did not feel she would be very good at "rapping." When she was informed that her name was high on the students' list of teachers they would like to work with, she almost cried. Until then she had not realized that she had achieved a lifelong ambition to be a "real" teacher and a "real" person. "One of the oldies with the goodies" was the phrase a student used in suggesting her as one of the most wanted volunteers.

"Seek, above all, for a game worth playing. Such is the advice of the oracle to modern man. Having found the game, play it with intensity—play as if your life and sanity depended on it. (They *do* depend on it.) Follow the example of the French existentialists and flourish a banner bearing the word 'engagement'. Though nothing means anything and all roads are marked 'NO EXIT', yet move as if your movements had some purpose. If life does not seem to offer a game worth playing, then *invent one.*" This is the note on which Robert S. De Ropp opened his most recent book, *The Master Game—Beyond the Drug Experience* (Dell Publishing Co.), written to remind adults that life is continually growing or it leads to the worst sort of death, that of the spirit.

DeRopp's advice is to get the best teacher you can find, until finally the player becomes the *magisterissimus* (the most superlative of teachers).

Richard H. Blum suggests that "we are all educators," and if one reads between the lines a bit, an educator is anyone dedicated to the development of people that others will want to emulate. The key word is "dedicated."

. . . I think the course best open to us in dealing with student drug use is that to which we are —in conjunction with our students—dedicated. That is education. We are all educators and we must have great hopes for knowledge as a means of guiding lives or we would not be in the business. Why not then remain consistent to our calling and to our beliefs and emphasize fact-finding and information-giving as means to acquaint students with the significance and effects of exotic drug use? We can also be aiming, as we do in much of education for civilization, at the development by students themselves of group norms and inner standards which sensibly guide their conduct.

I further suggest that educational efforts not be limited to students alone, but directed at the drug gatekeepers. Here I mean physicians, parents, pharmacologists in our laboratories, our campus professors and the graduate students. I suspect we shall find that with each new socially used drug these people will be the channels for learning attitudes, use, and sources of supply. If we want to have an impact we must talk to those who are models, those who are the opinion leaders for them —and that is as it must be—for education is a business of exchange, a dialogue, not a one-way street.

Richard H. Blum in his article, "Drugs and Personal Values," from the NIMH *Resource Book for Drug Abuse Education.*

Professional Ideas—Such as Listening

If you are a layman called upon to help a person with a drug problem, your best advice is likely to be, "get some professional help." Yet, many physicians do not feel qualified as counselors to young people with serious drug problems, and many other professionals have not been privy to the kind of knowledge and experience young people can appreciate. Another factor is the reluctance on the part of many who need it to seek counselling, and that may be why you have been singled out. There is something in you that has inspired a degree of confidence. Whatever your credentials, one particular quality is cherished by the person who talked to you, the art and grace of listening carefully.

Listening happens to be one of the responsibilities of growing up. A considerable distance in the "communication gap" is due to careless listening. We all know how much misunderstanding and human conflict are triggered by careless language.

Though the following selections were addressed to professionals who are especially concerned with listening carefully, laymen may benefit from some of the suggestions on technique.

Kenneth Keniston, Associate Professor of Psychiatry, Yale University, and a leading commentator and practitioner in counselling students about drugs, has warned that "it will not do to repudiate students who misuse drugs as moral lepers and addicts without trying to understand their motives for drug use, and the values and goals they pursue." These motives, he suggests, are a genuine, if misdirected search for "ultimate meaning and contact with the world." Dr. Keniston goes as far as saying that the drug user is "making a statement about how he wants to live his life."

. . . As for counseling student drug users—potential and actual—I think it important to acknowledge that the question of drug use is, in the last analysis, not a medical issue, but an existential, philosophical and ethical issue. Student drug users are, as a group, extremely knowledgeable about the possible bad effects of drug use; they can usually teach their counselors, deans and advisors a good deal about the potential bad side effects of drugs. They will argue—with considerable validity—that society does not prohibit the use of other psychoactive compounds (e.g., alcohol, tobacco) which in some ways are far more dangerous than many of the hallucinogens or amphetamines. In the last analysis, then, whether one chooses or not to use drugs in full consciousness of their possible bad effects and the legal implications of drug use, becomes an existential rather than a medical decision. It is a matter of how one chooses to live one's life, how one hopes to seek experience, where and how one searches for meaning. To be sure, I doubt that we can hope to persuade students that drugs are ethically, humanly or existentially undesirable if they are not already persuaded. But I think we can at least help the student confront the fact that in using drugs he is making a statement about how he wants to live his life. And we can, perhaps, in our own lives and by our own examples, suggest that moral courage, a critical awareness of the defects in our society, a capacity for intense experience and the ability to relate genuinely to other people are not the exclusive possessions of drug-users.

In the long run, those of us who are critical of student drug abuse must demonstrate to our students that there are better and more lasting ways to experience the fullness, the depth, the variety and the richness of life than that of ingesting psychoactive chemicals. Consciousness-expansion seems to me not the sole prerogative of psychoactive compounds, but of education in its fullest sense.

Thus, insofar as we can truly and honestly help our students to become educated in the fullest sense, we will be able to provide alternative routes to the pursuit of meaning, the quest for experience, and the expansion of consciousness. Obviously, much of what passes for education in America fails to accomplish any of these high objectives. As long as it continues to fail, I suspect that drugs will continue to be a problem on our campuses and in our society.

Dr. Kenneth Keniston in "Drug Use and Student Values," from the NIMH *Resource Book for Drug Abuse Education.*

Emergency Medicine, December, 1969, introduced a young man to it's readers, in an article, *The Trip There and Back*. The author, David E. Smith, M.D., was identified in a contributor's box as a "student of drugs and people."

As the founder and guiding spirit behind the Haight-Ashbury free clinic in California that now treats annually about 20,000 patients suffering from drug reactions and associated health problems, Dr. Smith has combined his experience and background in pharmacology and toxicology with his knowledge of the drug cult, and has become one of the most respected authorities in the field of drugs and alienated youth. During this phase of his life, in his early thirties, just a few years older than many of his patients, he is assistant clinical professor of toxicology at the University of California Medical Center, consultant on drug abuse to San Francisco General Hospital, and editor of the *Journal of Psychedelic Drugs.*

The following excerpt directs physicians to a problem in situation ethics. Dr. Smith's rationale is both humanistic and pragmatic.

I have been asked—and probably with complete sincerity—whether a physician *should* attempt to take the bumps out of a bad trip. Isn't a patient more likely to keep away from drugs in the future, the reasoning goes, if he has a bad trip the first time out? Certainly there *may* be some truth in this, but it's also true that an untreated panic reaction to LSD or other psychedelic drugs can lead to severe long-term psychological problems. There's also a very good chance of another residual effect. You've probably heard of "flashbacks"—the recurrence of the LSD experience days, weeks, or even months afterward without further use of the drug. These are primarily an aftereffect of a bad trip, and one of the principal reasons why proper treatment of an acute reaction to LSD or any of the other psychedelic drugs is so important.

Ethically, I think it's very questionable to let moral judgments influence the management of any emergency. In other areas of social disease—alcoholism and VD, for instance—this concept of humane, nonjudgmental treatment has been emphasized and is now generally accepted. But currently, the concern with increasing use of drugs, with their role in the youth culture of today, with their relationship to a generalized rebellion against the mores and practices of past generations, may obscure the point about proper medical practice as it applies to the acute drug reaction.

Even apart from the fact that the physician has a responsibility to do the best he can to help anyone who needs medical attention, you can do a better job in counseling the drug abuser about his long-range problems if you've taken care of him when he needed you.

When a patient has had a bad reaction to a drug and you've helped him through it, you've gone a long way toward gaining his trust, and you'll never find him more receptive to your advice and counsel. It would be naive of me to tell you that he'll not buy what you have to say one hundred per cent of the time, but he will listen while you point out—not sermonize on—the dangers of drug use and the problems he can get into, and suggest alternatives to a potentially destructive life style.

David E. Smith, M.D., in his article "The Trip There And Back," from *Emergency Medicine*, December, 1969.

"I swear by Apollo Physician, by Aesculapius, by Hygeia, by Panacea, and by all the gods and goddesses, making them my witnesses, that I will carry out, according to my ability and judgment, this oath and this indenture," begins the Physician's oath, followed by a list of excellent intentions, one of which is, "I will keep pure and holy both my life and my art."

Centuries later, if Apollo, Aesculapius, Hygeia, Panacea, or any other gods and goddesses interested in the struggle of the physician toward perfection had tuned in, they would have heard this prayer:

From inability to leave well alone, from too much zeal for what is new and contempt for what is old, from putting knowledge before wisdom, service before art, cleverness before common sense, from treating patients as cases, and from making the care of a disease more grievous than its endurance, Good God, deliver us. (Attributed to Sir Jonathan Hutchinson, an eighteenth-century British physician.)

Richard Burack, M.D., in *The New Handbook of Prescription Drugs.*

So far as we have looked into the likelihood, there is no counselor's oath comparable to the one Hippocrates prescribed for his practitioners. However, John H. Frykman, Director of drug treatment at the Haight-Ashbury Medical Clinic, has come close to describing what counseling should be ideally.

Counseling is helping a person help himself, not doing something for him.

Counseling proceeds on the basis of understanding, not by agreement or disagreement—communication is the byword.

Counseling provides clarification of issues and problems, but does not force someone into a "right" solution.

Counseling involves true respect for the other person, not the use of a clever bag of tricks, such as getting someone to cry, to respond, to open up.

When one begins to function as a counsellor, one should understand that to work with a person in a crisis is a real privilege. An obligation goes with this privilege: not to exploit the situation for one's own benefit. Many people get involved in "helping" others because of their own needs, rather than because of a healthy response to the plight of others seeking assistance. This is not to say that as counsellor you should ignore your own needs. In fact, you will probably understand the other person's needs better by experiencing the needs that he creates in you ("I'm afraid, because he admitted killing someone," or "He's in such bad shape, I wish I could take him into my home and take care of him"). Understand your own needs, but give priority to his. Then, as the counselling relationship develops, you can become a participant, working with him to draw out alternate solutions to particular problems.

The person seeking help also needs a certain understanding before effective counselling can begin. He must sense that something is wrong within himself, that he is not happy with his present state of affairs. He must also be willing to accept you as his counsellor, no matter what your qualifications or attitudes may be, and he must do this voluntarily. Nobody can be talked into doing anything about emotionally based issues, for reason does not apply to them, especially at the outset. Reason would say that a man should stop smoking because he has the first stages of lip cancer; but he can't listen to the reason, can't quit smoking, until he is willing to make a commitment about it at some deeper level. The use and abuse of psychoactive drugs is not a reasonable or rational form of behavior. For that matter, many common human problems are neither reasonable nor rational.

The person must also realize that his problem lies basically within himself, not in someone or something else. Too often a person blames his plight on a relationship that has gone bad or on drugs. When a person fills the air with "reasons" for his problems, these are only symptomatic of the underlying emotional disturbance and part of a systematic defense of his current station. The compulsive person can always see a reason for his plight—"If such and such hadn't happened some time ago, I would never have gotten myself into this situation." Such problems cannot be dealt with at the rational (thinking) level—they must first be met at the emotional (feeling) level, or not at all.

The person must feel free and safe in expressing his true feelings, without fear of how the counsellor will react. You can help him accomplish this in a number of ways:

1. by making it emphatically clear that you will keep all confidences as a sacred trust;
2. by offering help in such a way that it can be as easily refused as accepted;
3. by waiting patiently until he feels he wants to make the contact and identification with you— not forcing the relationship;
4. by concentrating on the articulated problems, despite becoming aware of far deeper ones;
5. by seeking to understand the problem not as you see it, but as he sees it;
6. by showing positive support of his struggle and interest in what he has to say, without necessarily agreeing with him at all times;
7. by not trying to solve things for him, instead helping him come to some conclusion about solving the problems himself;
8. by gently steering the conversation towards what he is obviously leaving out (usually on purpose), yet being careful not to second-guess him—not finishing sentences for him, for example;

9. by being aware that he probably senses or imagines what your response will be, because of his past experience with "helping people."

In short, by creating a climate of warmth, friendship, understanding, trust, rapport, and real communication—a climate which you do not contrive, but which you are careful not to upset by imposing on the person problems he may not yet be aware of ("I'm sure that many of your problems stem from . . ."), values you expect him to hold ("You really should try to . . ."), or things you expect him to do ("I want you to . . .").

Some guidelines for counselling

You, as counsellor, should not remain an outsider offering assistance. You must become a participant and work together with the person toward finding alternative solutions. Furthermore, it is imperative that you maintain respect for his integrity. If he happens to believe in "cosmological existentialism," you need not expect him to get over that "problem" before real progress can be made. Many counsellors today are not willing to accept a young, hip person's commitment to astrology. They feel compelled to convert him or to put down his belief, because they mistakenly see it as part of the problem.

You will soon notice that the "drug problem" usually drops out of the conversation very quickly. The drug is only incidental to the problem, and the problem is often similar to many of the human conflicts we experience in ourselves and in others. Usually the first things a person talks about are not the ones which really bother him. He needs to protect those for a while, until he feels secure and trusts you. One way in which you may begin to draw him out is to help him articulate his subconscious, to talk openly about the existence of that deeper level of reality: "I heard what you just said, but it seems to me there is something more important behind your words which I can't quite make out."

Be permissive—let him talk about anything he wishes, no matter how objectionable it may seem to you. Listen attentively, with understanding, sympathy, and acceptance. Be alert to requests for information and expressions of feelings about other people; these may help you understand what he is continually running up against. Listen without criticism and without interrupting his train of thought. Remember that arguments do not settle emotional problems. Even when you are listening, keep your part alive with "uh-huh . . . oh, yes . . . hmmm . . . is that so? . . ." and so on. Be open, relaxed, friendly.

Be empathetic—try to feel the way he is feeling, to project your own consciousness into his emotions, so that you acquire a personal sense of "where his head is at." Refrain from making verbal claims that you "know just how he feels," however. Accept his feeling and attitudes at face value, without continually questioning his motivation. Instead, reflect on what he has said after the fact, without interrupting because of your own anxieties.

Admit your ignorance about information he is trying to communicate. When you don't understand, ask him to explain; don't let it go by, thinking that you'll pick up on it through the total context of what he is saying. When you ask questions, ask them eductively, drawing him out rather than adding your opinion. If he says, for instance, that he is a good-for-nothing dope fiend, don't respond "Yes, it is really pretty bad to be a drug addict," but rather "Why do you feel that you are no good?"

Use his vocabulary as much as possible, and steer clear of your own favorite phrases, for these may be unintelligible to him. Avoid in particular any psychological, sociological, or other technical terms. For example, instead of "Are you having feelings of hostility?" try "Do you feel angry towards anyone right now?"

Avoid placing him in the position of having no way out. Ultimatums are never part of a good counselling situation, nor of any good human relationship, for that matter. When you make absolute demands you are telling about your needs, not listening to his.

Inquire about his previous experience with counselling. If it is broad, he may easily become a "professional mental patient," telling you in precise technical terms about his hang-ups while avoiding his pressing problems. Often a drug-oriented person will use this approach to get the specific limited response he seeks, such as medical help for withdrawal, lodging, food, or money, while unwilling to face the underlying causes of his problem and to change his life style.

Decide at the outset how many times you plan to see him, and let him know. It can be dangerous for both parties to feel that the weekly sessions (sometimes more frequent) might continue indefinitely. By telling him that you can probably meet eight or nine times, you let him realize that he cannot afford to procrastinate, that he really has to do business with himself if he is to take advantage of your help. By establishing such a limit, you also keep from getting entangled in your own needs. Some counsellors prefer the sessions to linger because it makes them feel good to have many people depending on them, or because it allows them to lay aside other more tedious work while feeling self-righteous ("I have X-number of people whom I am counselling weekly, and they need me"). After a few sessions it should be fairly clear how things are going, and, if warranted, a few extra sessions can be added.

Similarly, at the beginning of each session set a limit on its length (We'll have about an hour to talk"). When the end approaches, a gentle reminder may be in order ("We have about ten minutes left"). It is amazing how often a person brings up what is really bothering him in those closing moments.

Try to lead him into taking some concrete action about his problem before the interview is over —plan something on which to follow through. Summarize what has happened and make some arrangement (if it seems appropriate) for another contact. . . .

John H. Frykman in *A New Connection: An Approach To Persons Involved In Compulsive Drug Abuse.*

When Do You Start?

Parents and other teachers of small children have the best opportunities to shape the child's future. The patterns of behavior developed in childhood can determine, to a great degree, the kind of behavior the person will exhibit in later life. Evidence continues to accumulate on the powerful effects of early childhood experiences on the adult person.

The suggestions that follow, from a team of teachers from Marin County, California, are succinct enough to fit on the kitchen or classroom bulletin board.

Teaching Strategies Relating to Drug Education

Certain personality characteristics have been observed in young people who have abused drugs. These individuals have generally been described as showing or having shown problems in communication, passivity and low frustration tolerance, lag in social development, qualities of emptiness and apathy, to be isolates, poor relationships with peers, and to be exploitive of adults, impoverished in inner resources, and desirous of outside stimulation. Further, it has been noted repeatedly that the recurring cry from children is adult failure to accord them dignity and to be honest with them. Accordingly, optimum teaching strategies should aim to foster development of the whole child through such precepts as the following:

1. Avoid producing guilt, which acts to reduce one's sense of personal worth. Encourage free verbal expression of any emotion.

2. Accept emotion. Emotions are real and compelling. Suggesting alternative ways of handling crisis situations is preferable to suppression or repression of vividly experienced feelings. Discussion of such feelings is advantageous.

3. Know the child. Efforts made to become personally acquainted with the child will be invaluable. Acquaintance with the parents of each child helps in this understanding. It is worth keeping in mind that older children have complained repeatedly and bitterly that they experienced a loss of individuality in their school experience.

4. Encourage choices. The act of making decisions is something in which children could use much more practice than they get; opportunities for affording this are infinite. For example, "Do you want the blue paper or the red paper?" or "Do you want to do this problem or that one?," etc. Such activity is important in the development of a feeling of individual worth.

5. Be self-aware. Awareness and acceptance of one's own temperament and style sets a valuable example to children. It is no more desirable for the teacher to be depersonalized than

for the child. By being himself, the teacher sets an example—teaches by precept—a great lesson in self-acceptance.

6. Know your rights. It is a corollary to #5 to teach by precept that one can demand one's own rights in situations. The child cannot take all the teacher's attention, nor all of the teacher's time, nor does he really want it though he may try to get it. A teacher will help the child by assisting him in finding limits in his demands on the teacher's time as well as by setting limits on behavior.

7. Imaginary adventures and excursions. Such activity is useful in developing inner resources as well as helping children to distinguish between objective and subjective reality. Such activities (which may be based on actual experience, musical experience, a picture, etc.) should not be confined only to Kindergarten, but should be enjoyed throughout the primary grades.

8. Perception—broadly and intensively considered, multi-sensory. Increasing work is being done in visual perception, but this can be greatly expanded and enriched. Experiences in perceiving and reporting what is seen, heard, tasted, smelled or touched and kinesthetic experiences of lifting, pushing, pulling, etc.—all these contribute to a sense of selfness.

9. Learning to evaluate—this activity cannot be begun too early. Children need to become critics in the present-day world with its onslaught of stimulating experiences. Discussion of TV shows and their accompanying commercial messages is one method of encouraging evaluations.

10. Role-playing and creative drama—the experience of putting oneself in someone else's shoes as well as imagining situations helps in the child's development of his own individualism.

11. Appreciation of learning. Review with a child of the things he has learned and of their possible usefulness or relevance to his life helps to place them in a meaningful and favored con-text. Corollary to this, it might be commented that explanations to children prior to teaching them something—a unit or skill, for example—can give a child more reason for trying to learn the material than simply presenting material to be learned because the teacher ordains it.

12. Including the student in the evaluation portion of a parent conference gives him knowledge of what is said and opportunity to contribute. This may help to allay possible feelings of insecurity or guilt in the child.

"Program Recommendations for Elementary Teachers," from the **NIMH** *Resource Book for Drug Abuse Education.*

Something needs to be said here about the future, not next year's drug education program, but the condition in which man might find himself a decade or a generation or more hence. If we are right in saying that people, not drugs, are the problem, then the long way out probably will be found in cultivating the belief that one's own person and life are valuable, and therefore that good health is more to be desired than a chemical "high." The most widely acceptable condemnation that can be levelled against the abusive use of a substance is that it is unhealthy.

Perhaps through drugs themselves we will become the beneficiaries of a way to ease the torment of drug abuse. Some new substance, may alter human nature so that we might not require any other drugs.

Yet it seems wise to look, as some have done, for surer ways of understanding and dealing with human nature. The late psychologist, Abraham Maslow, drew the attention of our generation to what he called "peak experiences," those moments and hours in the life times of many people in which the most intense feelings and sometimes the most creative works occur.

Late in life Maslow took up the matter of human nature and health. Near ecstasy himself with the potential he found for man and saw for man's future, he described his vision of people undergoing personal growth leading to healthy human beings in an ever-healthier culture.

There is now emerging over the horizon a new conception of human sickness and of human health, a psychology that I find so thrilling and so full of wonderful possibilities that I yield to the temptation to present it publicly even before it is checked and confirmed, and before it can be called reliable scientific knowledge.

The basic assumptions of this point of view are:

1. We have, each of us, an essential biologically based inner nature, which is to some degree "natural," intrinsic, given, and, in a certain limited sense, unchangeable, or, at least, unchanging.

2. Each person's inner nature is in part unique to himself and in part species-wide.

3. It is possible to study this inner nature scientifically and to discover what it is like—(not *invent* —*discover*).

4. This inner nature as much as we know of it so far, seems not to be intrinsically or primarily or necessarily evil. The basic needs (for life, for safety and security, for belongingness and affection, for respect and self-respect, and for self-actualization), the basic human emotions and the basic human capacities are on their face either neutral, pre-moral or positively "good." Destructiveness, sadism, cruelty, malice, etc., seem so far to be not intrinsic but rather they seem to be violent reactions *against* frustration of our intrinsic needs, emotions and capacities. Anger is *in itself* not evil, nor is fear, laziness, or even ignorance. Of course, these can and do lead to evil behavior, but they needn't. This result is not intrinsically necessary. Human nature is not nearly as bad as it has been thought to be. In fact it can be said that the possibilities of human nature have customarily been sold short.

5. Since this inner nature is good or neutral rather than bad, it is best to bring it out and to encourage it rather than to suppress it. If it is permitted to guide our life, we grow healthy, fruitful, and happy.

6. If this essential core of the person is denied or suppressed, he gets sick sometimes in obvious ways, sometimes in subtle ways, sometimes immediately, sometimes later.

7. This inner nature is not strong and overpowering and unmistakable like the instincts of animals. It is weak and delicate and subtle and easily overcome by habit, cultural pressure, and wrong attitudes toward it.

8. Even though weak, it rarely disappears in the normal person—perhaps not even in the sick person. Even though denied, it persists underground forever pressing for actualization.

9. Somehow, these conclusions must all be articulated with the necessity of discipline, deprivation, frustration, pain, and tragedy. To the extent that these experiences reveal and foster and fulfill our inner nature, to that extent they are desirable experiences. It is increasingly clear that these experiences have something to do with a sense of achievement and ego strength and therefore with the sense of healthy self-esteem and self-confidence. The person who hasn't conquered, withstood and overcome continues to feel doubtful that he *could*. This is true not only for external dangers; it holds also for the ability to control and to delay one's own impulses, and therefore to be unafraid of them.

Observe that if these assumptions are proven true, they promise a scientific ethics, a natural value system, a court of ultimate appeal for the determination of good and bad, of right and wrong. The more we learn about man's natural tendencies, the easier it will be to tell him how to be good, how to be happy, how to be fruitful, how to respect himself; how to love, how to fulfill his highest potentialities. This amounts to automatic solution of many of the personality problems of the future. The thing to do seems to be to find out what one is *really* like inside, deep down, as a member of the human species and as a particular individual.

The study of such self-fulfilling people can teach us much about our own mistakes, our shortcomings, the proper directions in which to grow. Every age but ours has had its model, its ideal. All of these have been given up by our culture; the saint, the hero, the gentleman, the knight, the mystic. About all we have left is the well-adjusted man without problems, a very pale and doubtful substitute. Perhaps we shall soon be able to use as our guide and model the fully growing and self-fulfilling human being, the one in whom all his potentialities are coming to full development, the one whose inner nature expresses itself freely, rather than being warped, suppressed, or denied.

The serious thing for each person to recognize vividly and poignantly, each for himself, is that every falling away from species-virtue, every crime against one's own nature, every evil act, *every one without exception records itself* in our unconscious and makes us despise ourselves. Karen Horney had a good word to describe this unconscious perceiving and remembering; she said it "registers." If we do something we are ashamed of, it "registers" to our discredit, and if we do something honest or fine or good, it "registers" to our credit. The net results ultimately are either one or the other—either we respect and accept ourselves or we despise ourselves and feel contemptible, worthless, and unlovable. Theologians used to use the word *"accidie"* to describe the sin of failing to do with one's life all that one knows one could do.

This point of view in no way denies the usual Freudian picture. But it does add to it and supplement it. To oversimplify the matter somewhat, it is as if Freud supplied to us the sick half of psychology and we must now fill it out with the healthy half. Perhaps this health psychology will give us more possibility for controlling and improving our lives and for making ourselves better people. Perhaps this will be more fruitful than asking "how to get *unsick*."

How can we encourage free development? What are the best educational conditions for it? Sexual? Economic? Political? What kind of world do we need for such people to grow in? What kind of world will such people create? Sick people are made by a sick culture; healthy people are made possible by a healthy culture. But it is just as true that sick individuals make their culture more sick and that healthy individuals make their culture more healthy. Improving individual health is one approach to making a better world. To express it another way, encouragement of personal growth is a real possibility; cure of actual neurotic symptoms is far less possible without outside help. It is rela-

tively easy to try deliberately to make oneself a more honest man; it is very difficult to try to cure one's own compulsions or obsessions.

Abraham H. Maslow in his introduction to *Toward a Psychology of Being*.

"What are you going to do tonight, Marty?" (Paddy Chayefsky). If Marty were still wondering what he was going to do on the night of June 17, 1966, he might have tuned in on radio station KPFA, Berkeley, California, and picked up a few suggestions. For others who missed Henry Anderson's commentary, "The Case Against the Drug Culture" that night, we quote the following excerpts.

. . . I will describe a few things some friends and I have been experimenting with, off and on for a year or so, which seem to me to represent an alternative path to "consciousness expansion." This path doesn't require medical supervision. It doesn't involve going out of your mind. It is available to anyone who really wants to "turn on" without artificial props and assistive devices.

Unstructure groups of from two to twenty of us have come together from time to time, and here are just a few of the things we've tried:

1. Improvisatory scenes. Someone may start, for example, by saying: "This is a doctor's office. Somebody be the doctor; somebody be the nurse-receptionist; the rest of us will be patients. I'm an old man, waiting with not too much patience. . . ." Or someone may say, "I feel like being a politician running for office, about to go before the television cameras. Anybody care to be my opponent and debate me on the black-eyed pea issue?" Someone may take him up on it, and it goes from there until it stops being fun. Sometimes it doesn't work, but sometimes it turns out to be more hilarious than anything I've seen professional improvisers do. Nothing is funnier than the humor you, yourself, create; more beautiful than the beauty you create; or more heartbreaking than your own tragedies.

2. We've tried a lot of things to expand the uses of the voice, such as a kind of *a capella* choir in which everyone chooses a sound he considers right for him—for example, "boom, boom," for a bass; "twinkle twinkle, little star" for a soprano. One person volunteers as a conductor, and under his direction, we enter on cue, increase or diminish volume, accelerate or decelerate tempo, stop entirely, re-enter, and so forth. We often get remarkable effects.

3. Free body movement to music. We've usually used classical music, but it's sometimes swing, rock 'n roll, or experimental. The movement is whatever the individual is moved by the music to do: involving any or all parts of the body; involving or not involving other people; with eyes open or eyes closed; whatever.

4. Creative cookery. On one occasion, somebody supplied a wide variety of olives, tomatoes, lettuce, and other salad ingredients of different sizes, hues, and textures. Everyone constructed his own idea of a utopian salad. On another occasion, we were provided with a variety of ingredients for making soups—three hot soup bases, and twenty or more spices, condiments, and garnishes. On such occasions, we end by eating each other's handiwork—and there haven't yet been any fatalities.

5. With a simple 8-millimeter Bell and Howell camera, some indoor film, and photoflood lights, we once made our own "high camp" movie, with a hero, masquerading as a dissolute playboy, locking wits and brawn with a mad scientist.

6. We've had a lot of fun trying to assume the attributes and movements of familiar objects. For example, have you ever pretended you were an egg being broken, dropping into a pan, and frying? Or a vacuum cleaner, or an osterizer, or any number of other everyday things? One time, eight of us made up the component parts of an internal combustion engine, and it was the only machine I've ever felt any real enthusiasm for.

We've tried our hands at creating our own *musique concrete*, haiku, collages, clay modelling, finger painting, murals constructions of everything from IBM cards to the shoes on our feet. There are any number of uses of light, incense and other fragrances, the sense of touch, and so forth, that we've thought of but haven't had a chance to try yet.

We haven't spent any time sitting around intellectualizing. We've found the substance of liberation so exciting we haven't bothered with the theory. In my judgment, instead of finishing this article, you would do better to get up right now, move around, and start getting in touch with the space in the room, the textures of the walls, the floors, the drapes, all the things you've become deadened to and take for granted—most of all, yourself. But, in case anybody doesn't follow this precept, and is still reading, I'll violate my own advice and do some theorizing. I'm speaking only for myself, by the way, since my friends and I have not discussed these matters.

I think we've been proceeding on the assumption that in our compartmentalized, routinized lives, all of us have all kinds of capacities we've never used, and we've become afraid to even try to use them, for fear we'll "fail," or be laughed at. Timothy Leary, the high apostle of LSD, says most people go through life using perhaps five per cent of their potential consciousness, and I have no reason to doubt that he's quite right. That is the common kernel of truth from which Leary and his friends have been proceeding in one direction, and my friends and I in another altogether.

I and my friends, I think, have been assuming that the way authentically to expand the consciousness is to work on strengthening and developing the constituent elements which make up consciousness: the five basic senses; memory, imagination; the feeling for color, design, humor, and so forth and so on. The way you develop these things, I think, is to exercise them—to practice, very hard, the way a person, by working hard enough, may eventually be able to run a mile in less than four minutes. I don't believe there is any short cut, any easy way, in one kind of human development any more than the other.

You may have heard this joke: one person says "Have you got color TV?" The other person says, "No, I take LSD and sit and watch the wallpaper instead." In a real sense, that joke illustrates the point I am trying to make. I don't believe anyone's potentialities are really expanded by any amount of sitting around watching TV, no matter how good the color, the acting, the direction, etc. And I do not believe anyone's potentialities are really expanded by any amount of hallucinating on LSD, no matter how good the color of those visions. There is no substitute, no way I know of to really start using that 95 per cent of unused potential other than doing it yourself: mixing and applying your own colors, to paper or canvas or whatever; writing your own scripts; moving your own body; using your own voice; and all the rest of it.

My friends and I have found, I think, that in an appropriate interpersonal setting, it is possible to do these things. It is possible to be unafraid, to let go, to start a veritable freshet of seeing things in new ways—and through it all to know that our consciousness expansion is real, and not a dream, because it is shared, observed, communicated, and can be built upon at any later time.

The interpersonal setting in which we have found all kinds of creative capacities can emerge and flower is characterized by certain qualities: it is essentially unstructured, accepting, non-coercive, non-competitive, non-striving, non-judgmental, non-directive. There is no "purpose" in the usual sense. For example, we try not to let our gatherings become psychotherapy sessions. This is not to say they are not psychotherapeutic. In lives which are lived at the five or ten per cent level, *any* experience which is liberating, humanizing, and authentic

might legitimately be called psychotherapeutic. But that is a side-effect.

We have no leaders and no followers. We have no agendas. It is not necessary that everyone arrive at the same time, or leave at the same time. The closest thing we have to a rule, I suppose, is that no one shall laugh at anyone else. *With*, yes; but not *at*. The concepts of "success" and "failure" simply do not apply....

... It is very difficult to work our way out of the fear that we are going to be judged and found wanting if we step out of our narrow roles of housewife, or teacher, or whatever, and stretch our bodies, our minds, our voices, our talents in unaccustomed ways. But on the basis of my own experience, I can testify that it is possible. It's not mechanical. It's not something you work on all the time. You can put it aside, and take up later where you left off. But in the meantime, you know that it's there, and that is a very wonderful, reassuring feeling. It's very reassuring to know that you did it yourself, with your own powers; to know that the supply can't be cut off, government can't outlaw it, no force in the world can take away from you your accomplishment, or your ability to go on from it to similar accomplishments....

I like to believe that there is no discontinuity between the things my friends and I have done in seeking to enhance our creativity, spontaneity, and joy in life, and the things we may be doing in the social, political, economic arenas. I like to believe there is no inconsistency between social responsibility and one's responsibility to be one's self.

At the very least, I would say that the kinds of things we have been talking about here are refreshing, and to that extent make it possible to return with renewed effectiveness to grapple with the woes of the world. But I think there is more to it than that. I like to believe there is an organic and mutually reinforcing connection between the courage it takes to try a new kind of singing, dancing, painting, or play-acting, and the courage it takes to challenge an entrenched social institution. I like to believe there is a very real relationship between the kind of growth and liberation we are groping for in our own personalities and the kind of liberation all men deserve and all men are capable of....

"The Case Against the Drug Culture," by Henry Anderson from the Journal, *MANAS*, Nov. 16, 1966.

It has been almost two generations since William Whyte called attention to the streetcorner society, a now rapidly evolving phenomenon which has spread in new forms from slums to all of the places where American young people say they are at. Evenings and Sundays they gather at the empty shopping centers, and seated on the sidewalks of the main streets, they wait for something to happen.

Chapter Five

WHAT CAN SCHOOLS DO?

Probably the best way to start a discussion of what schools can do about drug abuse is to take a look at schools as they now are, and at what we want them to be.

. . . It is not possible to spend any prolonged period visiting public school classrooms without being appalled by the mutilation visible everywhere —mutilation of spontaneity, of joy in learning, of pleasure in creating, of sense of self. The public schools—those "killers of the dream" to appropriate a phrase of Lillian Smith's—are the kind of institutions one cannot really dislike until one gets to know them well. Because adults take the schools so much for granted, they fail to appreciate what grim, joyless places most American schools are,

how oppressive and petty are the rules by which schools are governed, how intellectually sterile and esthetically barren the atmosphere, what an appalling lack of civility obtains on the part of teachers and principals, what contempt they unconsciously display for children as children.

Schools can be humane and still educate well. They can be genuinely concerned with gaiety and joy and individual growth and fulfillment without sacrificing concern for intellectual discipline and development. They can be simultaneously child-centered and subject- or knowledge-centered. They can stress esthetic and moral education without weakening the three R's. They can do all these things if—but only if—their structure, content, and objectives are transformed.

Charles E. Silberman in *Crisis in the Classroom.*

Policies, Precedents and Procedures

According to a study reported in the October, 1967 issue of *NEA Journal*, state legislatures have set up more requirements for teaching children about alcohol and narcotics than any other topic. At the time George D. Marconnit conducted the study for the Iowa Center for Research in School Administration, forty-three states required such courses.

If attempts to control alcoholism by legislation and education have not achieved notable success, and the alcoholic statistics have not shown a dramatic response to lessons taught in classrooms, just what can we expect of the schools in the current drug crisis?

There is evidence that state legislatures have started to shift the focus from trying to legislate the drug problem out of existence through passage of more laws, to serious attempts to develop comprehensive, long-term programs with schools participating, but not solely responsible for educational programs. In 1970, for instance, the General Assembly in Colorado passed legislation for a community education program to reach members of the various health professions, students, educational institutions, parents, and the community at large. An interdepartmental task force on alcohol and drug abuse was set up to formulate, implement, and evaluate the program. Among the committee's recommendations, it encouraged school districts to shift their emphasis from traditional topics and teaching methods to the study of people and their needs. Other state legislatures seem to be realizing that traditional methods of teaching about drugs are useless. A special supplement of *Compact*, December, 1970, published by the Education Commission of the States, reports on the status and direction of drug education in the states. (See Appendix, page 99.)

Whatever the laws or appropriations passed by legislative bodies, the cutting edge of action and change is felt in schools through the decisions of school boards and administrators. These are the people with authority and responsibility who outline policies, and who determine the educational programs and practices. This seems to be the case in both the large urban systems and the small rural districts. What the schools can do about drugs, therefore, tends to start with policies made by school boards, although the attitudes of individual members may sharpen and hasten decisions made by boards.

For several years a number of professionals have been working on educational policies related to the prevention of drug abuse, and their conclusions and suggestions may be quite valuable to boards and administrators now developing or revising their own attitudes and guidelines toward school programs.

In the formation of educational policy, careful consideration should be given to the recommendations of professionals and to conclusions reached by responsible groups who have addressed similar issues. Administrators developing or revising policy guidelines may find the following suggestions and observations useful.

. . . School policies which punish rather than support, alienate rather than enlist, frustrate rather than hearten, injure rather than pardon, and provide darkness rather than light, are calamities.
. . . The school program must begin early. It is no longer appropriate to conceive of drug abuse education as a unit or course only at the secondary level.
. . . The best deterrent to drug abuse is the [development of a value system in the child that will aid him in assessing the consequences of all forms of drug use.]
. . . Drugs per se are not the issue; rather, the issue is why people use them.
. . . Exaggeration, distortion, and sensationalism are propaganda, not education, and have no place in the school.
. . . It is important that they [parents and community] be convinced that the school plays but one part in the total effort. . . .

Marvin R. Levy, in "Guidelines for Drug Programs," U.S. Senate Hearings before the Special Subcommittee on Alcoholism and Narcotics, September, 1969. (Excerpt slightly simplified.)

If our goal is prevention, then the basic target population should be present "nonusers" of drugs.
. . . it is part of the educational process that a clearcut understanding of the penal laws on dangerous drugs be brought to the attention of students. They should be aware of the degree of severity of

these penalties and the difficulties which may come to them when these laws are broken, such as difficulty in getting into a college, to find a job, to go into a profession, and to obtain a civil service position.

Robert Dolins, Assistant Commissioner, New York State Narcotic Addiction Control Commission, in "Misuse and Abuse of Drugs," from the *Journal of the New York State School Boards Association, Inc.*, March 1969.

The teacher . . . [can] have a great influence on the decision to take or continue to take drugs. . . . He may be able to persuade his pupil by presenting factual information. This is no taboo topic. If reliable information about drugs is not obtained, questionable information will be gathered from street myths. . . .

It seems reasonable to insist that usage or trafficking of any illegal drug not be permitted on school grounds.

Sidney Cohen in *The Drug Dilemma.*

The unwise exercise of adult authority in its attempt to break the connection of youth and drugs may have negative effects. . . .

The adult task is to help the young to assist each other resist the temptation of drugs. They must trust that our youngsters can and will reject drug abuse. The desire of the young to be active, involved, committed, and to have responsibility, sounds through our society at every turn. We know of no more important issue on which the claim for participation and responsibility can be better earned than in youths' assumption of leadership in solving the drug problem.

Regents of the State University of New York, **Press Release, February 27, 1970.**

The New York State Education Department issued Guidelines for School Programs for the academic year starting in September, 1970, prepared with the assistance of Donald E. Barnes, from which the following passage on school district policies and procedures has been selected.

There are certain basic concepts and approaches which should occur in every school district's program to prevent drug abuse. These are, briefly:

Boards of education should adopt written policy on programs relating to the prevention of drug abuse as they do with other programs. These should include a clear statement of their concern and the priority they assign to this problem as well as a statement of their policy in regard to a district-wide curriculum, pupil services for drug users, and additional staff responsibilities. School boards are advised to organize advisory committees which include students, teachers, and parents in developing policy and procedures. A statement should be included which clearly specifies the staff responsibilities in instances of suspected and known drug use by students.

Boards of education, by their statement of policy, will set the tone for the whole drug abuse prevention program. A concerned expression of their desire to assist students to face and successfully cope with the attractions of drug abuse is to be encouraged. This can be demonstrated by the responsible involvement of youth in the development of policies and procedures. The board's support and concern for the importance of the serious nature of the drug abuse prevention program will be demonstrated by their budgeting and staff support. The superintendent, assisted by his school administrators, is faced with responsibility of implementing the policies and procedures established by the board of education.

Many students are acutely aware of the real dangers associated with drug abuse. Their friends, classmates, and they themselves, are faced with decisions on whether to experiment with drugs and when to stop experimenting. A successful drug program must arouse the student's concern for drug abuse and mobilize that concern in constructive ways. School administrators should *develop programs* and mobilize staff in ways to help students develop their own reasonable solutions, rather than arbitrarily to impose adult solutions.

Early and responsible *involvement of students* is extremely important. There are certain natural leaders in the student population who frequently are not associated with established student organizations. These students, who are generally known to both staff and students, frequently exert considerable influence on small peer groups. Natural leaders who are against drug use can contribute a great deal to a school prevention program. Where no natural leader with these convictions can be identified, an intensive workshop to develop leadership skills can be provided in the district.

Teachers have opportunities and skills which could have a significant impact on a drug abuse prevention program. They meet regularly with students and are in a position to be aware early of potential drug problems. Relevant material in curriculum, classroom discussions, coordinated cooperation of teachers, and well-developed and integrated courses have a great deal of influence upon student attitudes.

The school's *relationship with local community agencies*, and particularly the police, should be worked out. The school's drug abuse prevention program should be thoroughly explained to all segments of the community. Whenever possible, students should be encouraged to take responsibility for some of the planning of these programs.

The *continuing education program* in a school district offers an excellent opportunity for involving parents and young adults in the school's drug abuse prevention program. An ongoing program can provide significant assistance to parents and the community in developing a successful drug program.

There is danger that many communities will organize and act decisively to discourage drug abuse and then lose interest when their campaign appears to be taking effect. The American experience with alcohol demonstrates an amazing tendency to look the other way and accept bad public health conditions.

Boards of education should recognize the need for continuing programs based on coordinated planning, so that well-qualified teachers can influence the development of students throughout their whole school career. When the aim is wholesome psychological and social growth, a continuing school program is indicated.

A *committee* to deal with drug abuse is a common approach in secondary schools in the State. These committees usually consist of a principal,

school physician, school nurse-teacher, school psychologist, school psychiatrist, school social worker, guidance counselor, and health education teacher. The addition of students as advisors should increase the effectiveness of such groups as a resource to administrators faced with difficult decisions concerning individuals.

From *Education's Role in the Prevention of Drug Abuse—Guidelines for School Programs*, The University of the State of New York, the State Education Department, 1970.

Regulations and Authority

The need for understanding student motivations and for encouraging student initiative and responsibility often causes specialists in drug education to lean toward permissiveness. Few of them, however, mean to advocate the breakdown of anything more in schools and colleges than mistrust and misunderstanding. Who among us does not recognize the need for good organization and for that fair use of authority which attracts respect and seeks to protect the rights of all?

. . . The phenomenon of turning on others presents high school and college administrators, as well as society as a whole, with a real quandary. If a benign attitude is adopted toward illicit users of drugs such as marihuana and LSD, many users will simply continue their involvement with drugs and go their own ways, but others will insist on devoting their energies to increasing the size of their drug sub-culture. Given an insouciant attitude on the part of a school administration, a proselytizing minority of 5 per cent could subvert the majority in short order. This in essence is what happened in England over the last five years regarding heroin use, and the result has been an increase of over 600 per cent in youthful heroin users in that country. It is happening in this country now with marihuana. The only sensible approach, it would seem, is for high schools and colleges to establish specific rules and regulations in regard to drug use and then to react vigorously when students are caught violating those regulations; for if the peer-group proselytizers are not forced to desist,

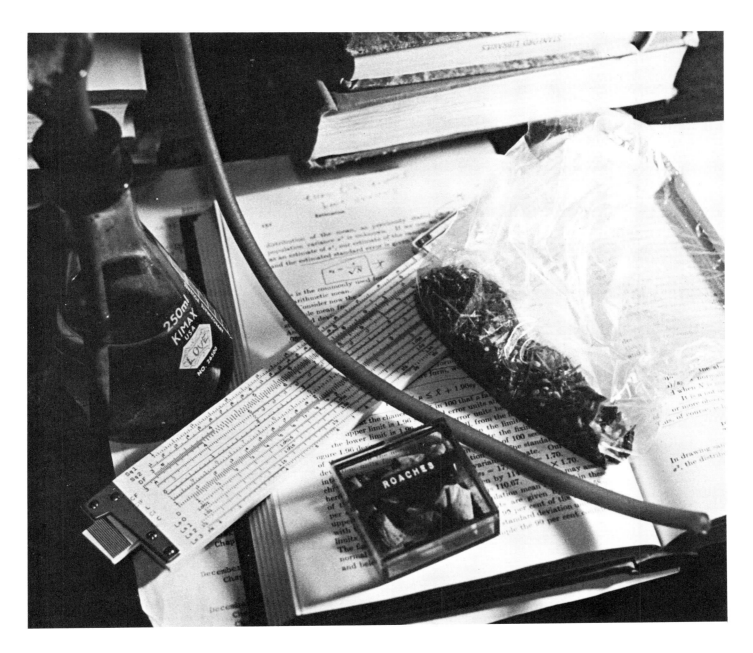

or removed from the environment, the situation will ineluctably get worse.

. . . Once regulations are established in regard to drugs, each institution must demand obedience, or it will encourage not only drug use but also a form of irresponsibility which inevitably will interfere with the learning process. More and more schools and colleges are adopting a firm but fair approach. Harvard College took the most publicized step in the spring of 1967. Their brief memo-

randum to the freshman class said, "As anyone bright enough to be at Harvard knows perfectly well, possession or distribution of marijuana and LSD is strictly against the law and taking drugs involves users in psychological dangers and contacts with the criminal underworld. The college is prepared to take serious disciplinary action up to and including dismissal against any student found to be involved in use or distribution of illegal and dangerous drugs. In sum, if a student is stupid enough to misuse his time here fooling around with illegal and dangerous drugs, our view is that he should leave college and make room for people prepared to take good advantage of the college opportunity."

To dismiss a student and thereby endanger his entire future is indeed a harsh penalty, but the obligation of schools and colleges is to consider the health of the community at large; to allow illicit drug users to remain active is to court disaster, in that they may well attempt to subvert as many of their classmates as possible. The Harvard approach is firm but allows the administration flexibility in dealing with each individual case.

Despite the need for a firm approach it is clear that caution must be exercised in regard to entrapment within our schools and universities. There is absolutely no reason for the college campus to be inviolate if students are disobeying the laws by illicit use or distribution of dangerous drugs, but by the same token it would be tragic if the drug problems in our educational institutions were compounded by paranoia relating to undercover agents within the student body. Since it stands to reason that the campus cannot be sancrosanct for the drug pusher, a reasonable compromise might mandate that the school administration always be informed of the presence of undercover agents and that the function of those agents be strictly limited to ferreting out and punishing those who are clearly involved in the sale of drugs. Although detection and arrest of users of drugs such as heroin and marihuana is also a police function, entrapment of users by undercover agents within the university environment would create far more problems than it would solve.

Whenever possible, much of the responsibility for coping with the illicit use of drugs in educational institutions should be relegated to student council organizations, since in both high schools and colleges student representatives are usually well motivated and highly responsible. They know the drug users as well as the drug proselytizers, and they are far more knowledgeable in this regard than any school administration. If they themselves will accept the responsibility for discouraging drug use on campus, the extent of abuse within those environments will rapidly diminish.

Donald B. Louria, M.D., in *The Drug Scene.*

The Realm of Affect

It should be emphasized that in school drug programs *what* is done seems to be less important than *how* it is done and by *whom.*

The evidence so far clearly indicates that education with respect to drugs must go far beyond delivery of information. It becomes necessary to build attitudes and concepts about life and the order of things. Students need time for that, and the adults concerned—policymakers, teachers, and parents—also need to examine their own attitudes and behavior.

The Committee for Psychedelic Drug Information proposed these changes in educational policies:

These proposals for changes in education are predicated on the assumption that such changes would discernibly decrease the causes which underlie alienation among youth. . . .

Educational programs which do not have an ethical basis do youth a definite disservice, and it would seem that educational programs today have tended to become more and more devoid of an ethical perspective. The educator is duty-bound to guide his students in the direction of the wisest possible choices. The educator can fulfill an important role by guiding his students in the direction of the highest values and ideals that he himself perceives. It is essential that education renew its focus upon the understanding and inculcation of ideals and goals. It is further essential that the lives of exemplary individuals and exemplary societies and civilizations, both Eastern and Western, be studied with such an objective in mind. Young people are looking for direction and purpose and the prescripts that they receive today have little or no relevance to their lives. Techniques of critical analysis have made us more inclined to take apart and to find fault with things rather than to approach problems and situations in constructive and creative ways. The educational process has failed if the young person leaves secondary school unable to cope in a constructive way with the problems which he faces. The educational process has failed if the young person has not developed a sense of direction and some basic values concerning what is right. . . .

Another most effective way of helping to change attitudes and stimulate thinking in innovative and creative directions is to utilize young persons in the schools as part of a program to awaken higher aspirations in the students. Efforts which have seemed effective have involved young persons (usually college age) who have surmounted problems currently confronting persons their own age and younger. The experiences they can share with students can be a means for providing some of the most significant educational experiences imaginable. It is essential that young persons who would be called upon to take part in school assemblies, class discussions, or group or individual counselling would have high ideals and would be capable of inspiring others to a richer and more meaningful life.

From *Proposed Changes in Educational Policies* by the Committee for Psychedelic Drug Information, Berkeley, California.

The late President Kennedy's Commission on Narcotics and Drug Abuse concluded, "An educational program focused on the teenagers is the *sine qua non* of any program to solve the social problem of drug abuse. . . . The education of the teenager is, therefore, an essential requisite of any preventive program." . . .

Every effort must be made to create an honest, free and open setting; a milieu in which a student may examine alternatives and make decisions so that his actions are those best for him and those he affects. If a climate of urgency is upon us, it must be redirected toward restructuring the school environment to make each student's experience relevant for him in terms of his needs, interests, and aspirations. . . .

The primary methodology by which real decisions are fostered is with simple group processes. Through this medium, all students will be provided with an increased awareness of the world around them. An awareness greater and more meaningful than the promise of mind expansion through drugs. . . .

Schools should provide teachers with time in the school day to discuss topics of mutual concern. No agenda, no curriculum, no structure is necessary, just time for free exchange of ideas. Starter questions can be developed to get the discussions rolling and as a springboard for meaningful encounters.

Schools would do well to provide a setting, not necessarily in the school building, where students can come to talk to each other and adults regarding matters of concern.

Finally, there must be wide-spread commitment on the part of the entire staff to create an open environment where boys and girls feel secure, wanted, loved, and free to express their innermost feelings. The school should be this kind of place. . . . Instead of being pompously critical of student drug abuse, we should demonstrate that there are better ways to experience the richness of living; ways better and less dangerous than ingesting chemicals. If we are truly to educate students in the fullest sense, we must help them to find other ways. The school must strive to develop the student as a human being capable of rational decision making, for in the final analysis, the decision still rests with the individual. . . .

Since personality is largely the cumulative effect of experience and since all experience has its effect, it is incumbent upon all of us to see that the whole atmosphere of the school is conducive not only to the physical well-being of boys and girls, but also to their mental health. . . .

Marvin R. Levy in *What Can Schools Do? A Time For Relevance*, a paper presented to the American Public Health Association, 96th Annual Meeting, Detroit, Michigan, November 12, 1968.

Jean Aron, of the Mental Health Department, Santa Clara County, California, in Hearings before the Special Subcommittee on Alcoholism and Narcotics, September, 1969, was quoted, "My feeling is that there are two basic principles which have to be accepted as bases for drug education with potential for success. . . . It is the responsibility of a school system to provide its instructors with all possible information about drugs and to create a climate for open discussion. An important fact of honesty in addition to straight facts is the willingness to say, 'I don't know' and 'let's find out.' "

One approach to drug abuse is the appointment of a full-time staff member to coordinate the drug abuse prevention program. This specialist should assist students in collection and management of an information library for students and faculty. He finds and screens outside resources which might be helpful in a school drug program. He advises administration and staff about drug problems and plans and leads workshops and in-service programs. He serves as the liaison with community drug programs and agencies, assisting with referrals and follow-up as needed.

The specialist's most important role, however, is in working with students in organizing their own prevention projects, in aiding communication between the students and faculty, and in counseling individuals and small groups of students.

The selection of a coordinator for a drug abuse prevention program should not be based upon identification with any specific profession, but should take into account personal qualities and desirable specialized training. The New York State Education Department and several institutions are offering special training programs to provide some of this training. There are some important considerations in this position.

1. It is essential that the coordinator be able to *relate effectively with students*. He should not be authoritarian or manipulative. He should have a high tolerance for ambiguous situations, accept student decisions, and respect the opinions of others. He should have acquired good counseling techniques and be capable of earning the trust and esteem of students. He may function informally with respect to administrative responsibilities.

2. *Trusting, professional relationships* should be offered to students. The specialist must be permitted considerable professional judgment in using the information he receives. He should maintain only the most essential records.

3. *Good staff relationships* are also very important. He must have an ability to attract the personal commitment of staff to the program and be able to encourage them to examine their own attitudes about drugs. At times the drug coordi-

nator will serve as an advocate for a student, and this role should be expected from him.

4. *School administration support* for the program and role of the specialist is essential. He should be relieved of responsibility to maintain liaison with police officials. His office, library, and meeting room should be readily accessible to both students and faculty. His professional relationships to students should be respected.

From *Education's Role in the Prevention of Drug Abuse—Guidelines for School Programs*, The University of the State of New York, the State Education Department, 1970.

Ira Frank, M.D., Neuropsychiatric Institute, University of California, Los Angeles, was asked, "How do you select the teachers to use in your program?" and "How do you get them when you're not in school; you don't know the teachers. There are some teachers who think the students like them, but the students don't."

Dr. Frank replied, "There are teachers that the students tend to hang around. They stay after class to talk to the teacher. The teacher usually shows a definite interest in them, attending extracurricular activities. You can spot these teachers in any school. We find them in two ways. They're referred to us by their principals in schools where there's a definite problem. Also, students come to them and ask them about drugs, and then the teachers get in touch with us directly."

From *Drug Addiction and Drug Abuse* (Selected Papers of a Seminar in Casper, Wy., Feb., 1969, for Wyoming Physicians. Western Interstate Commission for Higher Education, Boulder, Colorado, June, 1969).

. . . One of the most powerful barriers to staff-student communication is the LSD (and marijuana) user's fear of disclosure to enforcement authorities. In all states, students are subject to criminal prosecution for psychedelic use and are reluctant to approach counselors or administrators for help. In drug education and counseling, the promise of confidentiality is a powerful ally. Learn the laws in your state regarding privileged communication. If there is an undesirable possibility of confiscation of files, you might refrain from making written evidence of the student's drug involvement. From an enforcement point of view, the casual user is of minor importance compared with illicit manufacturers and distributors.

But whatever attitude toward disclosure you . . . adopt, it is of primary importance to make that policy explicit to the student body. Specifically, if an individual begins to present self-incriminating statements, he should be immediately advised of the degree of confidentiality that can be guaranteed. Bad faith, or "finking" on a student when policy is not explicit is disastrous for the overall objective. Honesty and openness of intent is critical.

To *tell* a student not to use LSD or marijuana is to convince him of nothing. Coercion works inversely with attitude change. Yet I have great faith in students' common sense and independent judgment. Provided they are given all the facts, the more they know about drugs, the less they will want to use them. Under this assumption, I propose the creation of a file library, or library section where written material relevant to drugs is available to students. The drug information center could contain publications placed on reserve which could circulate to interested individuals. . . . The collection might focus on two questions: "Are psychedelics worth it?" and "What are the alternatives to drugs?". . .

. . . Attitudes aside, the use, possession, and sale of psychedelic agents is against the law. Some of the penalties for conviction are, in practice, relatively mild; others are extremely severe. Your students need to know the laws and penalties attendant to drug use in your state and community. Some students are not aware of the gravity of drug convictions, especially the implications of a criminal record. It is true that mere knowledge of drug laws, especially considering the low probability of arrest, may not prove a significant deterrent. But it can be an important variable for realistic students.

Allan Y. Cohen, Ph.D., in "Psychedelic Drugs and the Student: Educational Strategies." (Originally in *Journal of College Student Personnel*, March 1969. Revised, 1970.) From the Committee for Psychedelic Drug Information, Box 851, Berkeley, California.

One of the most affecting statements in the literature of drug abuse prevention was made in a letter explaining the personal viewpoint of a private school headmaster. His letter states the case eloquently for an education that helps students learn to make their own decisions. Thus his argument illuminates the differences between those who would condition and control students and those, on the other hand, with enough courage to risk an educational process that allows students practice in making choices.

A trustee of the Latin School of Chicago sent to Headmaster Edwin S. Van Gorder a copy of the article "Turning Off: A Drug Drop-out Tells Why," by Allan Y. Cohen, published in the Chicago Sun-Times of April 13, 1969. Mr. Cohen, who is an assistant professor of psychology at John F. Kennedy University near Berkeley and is active as a consulting psychologist and in drug research, was one of the graduate students involved in the controversial research into psychedelic drugs conducted at Harvard in the early sixties by Drs. Timothy Leary and Richard Alpert. A former addict, Mr. Cohen now believes that drugs are useless and can be harmful. Mr. Van Gorder's response to the trustee is printed below.

DEAR MR. . . .

I have some objections to the approach of the article by Allan Y. Cohen which you sent me, as you may have anticipated. What he says is impressive and useful for a young person to consider and, in my opinion, his conclusion is the right one. The trouble is, he is making the conclusion for the youngster, rather than pointing out alternatives and relative risks. He says himself early in the article that it wasn't long ago that he was encouraging young people to adopt the opposite point of view from the one that he is now encouraging them to adopt.

Young people today beg us to "tell it like it is." I believe we are dealing with a sincere and not easily deceived group of youngsters.

One way to measure success when dealing with young people is to ask whether or not you have succeeded in indoctrinating them with your viewpoint. Another way is to ask questions like the following: Are they considering more alternatives? Are they better able to predict the outcomes of these alternatives? Are they gaining in confidence and in a sense of adventure and in an ability to recover from mistakes? The last point takes an added measure of courage, for it recognizes that in order to grow, youngsters *must* sometimes make mistakes and hold views different from our own, and this can be embarrassing to parents or headmasters. But I find that youngsters who are approached in this way, in fact, grow up to be less susceptible to propaganda from either side of any issue and altogether more realistic and desirable human beings than those who are successfully indoctrinated. And of course, indoctrination has its perils too, for many youngsters react so completely against the indoctrinated viewpoint, whatever it is, that they can never recover.

I wonder, in your own childhood, if you were exposed to people who were talking about "Hellfire" or the dangers of alcohol or cigarettes or of sexual activity outside a very narrow range. As is the case with most successful adults, I bet you had to work through some of those threats and attempts at indoctrination before you could really know what kind of person you were and how *you* chose to deal with the world. Drugs to young people today are an issue not unlike alcohol was when we were youngsters and, just as there were people then telling us, quite correctly, that alcohol could be the road to ruin, there are people now telling youngsters that drugs are the road to ruin. In point of fact, most kids know better than to be frightened into decisions. I truly believe that any youngster who tries anything stronger than pot is making a dreadful mistake, and I shall do anything in my power to help him reach a wise decision. But I am not going to exaggerate dangers or tell him what he must do in order to be an acceptable human being; I have no answers for him —only opinions that I hope he will consider. The last thing I want to do is to attempt to indoctrinate him and thereby either lose him through a reaction or, even worse, succeed and end up with another robot where a thinking, adventuresome person could have been.

I recall a Sunday evening church meeting for young people where the pastor said that he was going to consider all the major religions of the world absolutely impartially in the next two hours and then show why Christianity was best.

I tell youngsters that I consider experimenting with anything stronger than pot roughly in the category of playing Russian roulette, and that I

hope very much that they will not engage in such activities. At the same time, I tell them that this is only my viewpoint and that I certainly have changed my viewpoints about a lot of things through the years. It must be recognized that I might be wrong. The thing I want most for them to do is to consider the alternatives, to weigh consequences, and to come to their own decision. I also try to point out that there are some decisions in our lives which are critical decisions in that once made we lose alternatives or, at least, it becomes very difficult to place ourselves in a position where we have similar alternatives. Marriage is such a decision, as taking a job can be. So is the decision to drive recklessly, for all of a sudden one can find oneself in a position where the alternatives are all dreadful. And the same can apply to a decision to experiment with hard drugs.

Of course, it isn't feasible to behave exclusively in the way I have indicated. Many youngsters are so miseducated by the time they get to school that there is little hope for them at all beyond indoctrination. The demands of the moment or the needs of the organization may necessitate something like indoctrination. But I am convinced, nearly irrevocably, I'm afraid, that almost every time we refuse to recognize a youngster's predicament and the absolute necessity for him to make choices for himself, we are acting against his future. I should like to help him clarify the issue, to increase his understanding where possible, to help him recognize what risks are involved on either side of any issue he is considering, and finally to have him find the courage that is necessary to move ahead, being responsible for his own choice and recognizing the possibility that he may "screw up" and have to make costly readjustments in his life.

That is the remarkable thing about Mr. Cohen, isn't it? When he recognized that he was in trouble, he did readjust his life. And this is the lesson that I see as important for young people to grasp; not his particular issue or his view of the true and correct way to live—there are too many impressive other people who hold forth quite different views to young people to claim Mr. Cohen is THE EXPERT. Impressive, that is, to the young people, perhaps because of our ill-considered uses of mass media and our cultural peculiarities, which lead our youngsters into an eagerness to regard their peers and those somewhat older as knowledgeable and "in." These same cultural peculiarities tend to cast adults in general as slightly comic reactionaries. It is in assuming the role of the reactionary that we forfeit so many ball games that could at least have been well-fought contests. No more than anyone else have I a formula for saving youngsters from drugs, but I know *how* I *want* to take my losses, and this is not by a failure of fascistic indoctrination. Is it being too dramatic to suggest that you fought a war so that I could teach this way?

Sincerely,
EDWIN S. VAN GORDER, III
Headmaster
The Latin School of Chicago

Edwin S. Van Gorder in "Drugs: Letter to a Trustee," from *The Independent School Bulletin*, May, 1970.

Surely it is a commonplace to say that what schools can do and must do first is to be true to the idea for which they exist. In dealing with drug abuse it is crucial for a community to improve and fortify itself by providing its young people and their families with the best possible schools.

Everything we have read and every aspect of drug abuse prevention that we have examined points to the fact that the issues seem to be larger than drugs, and insofar as schools are concerned, the pivotal questions and answers have to do with the quality of the education offered and the extent to which the interests of students prevail.

Several school and community programs are described in the next chapter along with an account of our attempt to locate some of the country's outstanding drug prevention programs.

STANDARD
WHAT WILL TURN YOU ON ?
THIS OR THIS?
LSD
UPS
DOWNS
MARIJUANA
SPEED
WORK
FOOD
PLAY
FRIENDSHIP
EDUCATION
INVOLVEMENT
LOVE
THE LIFE YOU SAVE
ILL BE YOUR OWN
CLASS 6-508

Chapter Six

SCHOOL AND SOCIETY

Who is presumptuous enough to predict what patterns of drug behavior will predominate in the 1970's when he recalls the innocence of the populace when the 1960's began? Then "drugs" meant narcotics consumed mainly in New York City and to a minor extent in other cities, and in the slums for the most part.

But a series of cultural shockwaves traveled from Liverpool around the world, and those vibrations carried much more than the Beatles' powerful music. They transmitted a new culture which belonged almost exclusively at the outset to the young. By the late '60's, the language, dress, customs and arts of that new culture were flourishing at every crossroads in the United States, and at many other points and places in the world. Moreover, the new culture had its own visible and audible network for nearly instant communication of ideas, feelings, and experiences.

Late in the decade of the 1960's, to the consternation of nearly all adults, it became obvious that drugs had entered the social experience of an entire generation of adolescents and college-age youth. Drugs were no longer narcotics in slums and the underworld, but had instead come to mean barbiturates and amphetamines from the family medicine cabinet, psychedelics, and heroin smoked in army barracks by large numbers of American service men.

Those who attempt to interpret the drug experience of the 1960's in order to prepare for the 1970's will have to rely on sources at some distance from events. Of the demographic studies completed before and during the '60's, many were crudely done.

Studies and evaluations are in progress in virtually every state, and the task of keeping informed about what other people are doing or have done is a full-time job. A list of state legislative actions appears in the Appendix.

Whatever the outcome of pilot projects and evaluative studies in progress at this writing, it appears quite probable that schools will have to continue to try to help students who are experimenting with drugs, many of them at risk of death. And in all high schools and communities, without exception, children will be experimenting freely with alcohol and tobacco.

Educators obliged to respond to sudden community demand for new and intensified drug education programs will probably continue to feel misgivings. The public priorities have been assigned to medical treatment and attempted rehabilitation of narcotics addicts, while funds for research related to drug education have been lamentably scarce. Public demand for better educational programs has not been accompanied by fiscal support for training and employment of full-time drug specialists. The schools have had to shift for themselves in trying to aid the minority of students using hard drugs as well as the millions of nonaddicted students exposed to drugs other than narcotics.

Most educators are convinced of the soundness of long term approaches to drug education, and of the idea of helping children to develop inner strengths and values. Many educators, nevertheless, feel that they have to provide special instruction and other immediate assistance *now* for those students who are under pressure from peers, and who are drawn for many reasons toward the drug scene. But what kinds of instruction and assistance are needed? What works? Who is operating a program with demonstrated effectiveness? In what kinds of schools? What portions of such programs can be transferred to *our* schools? Such questions were being asked in nearly all American communities.

Such were the questions which led to a small survey conducted by the Institute for Educational Development in 1970, as part of the priorities assigned on behalf of two large high schools in New York City. At their request, IED, as educational consultants, undertook the task of trying to locate successful drug education programs which the client high schools might adopt or adapt.

Surveying "Noteworthy" Programs

The first stage of the survey was a review of the literature related to prevention of drug abuse. We found 44 school and community programs scattered through sixteen states. A few of the programs were mentioned in the course of conversations with bibliographic advisors. We made contact by letter and telephone with many of the programs and requested more information, usually supplied and in many cases generously. Most were obviously caught shorthanded, or short of cash to handle the sudden demand for information.

Later we faced the need for a more thorough survey based upon a more orderly selection process. First, we asked the U.S. Office of Education and the National Institute of Mental Health to identify persons in state agencies whom they considered judicious and well informed about school programs in their states. One official in each of 13 states was named. Thereafter, two rounds of interviews were necessary, both conducted by telephone.

In the first round we asked each of the contributors to identify the noteworthy programs in his or her state. We defined "noteworthy" to mean "outstanding in comparison to other programs, interesting in the sense of being innovative or unusual, and productive to the extent that the program showed promise of good results, even if the results had not been demonstrated, nor the program evaluated." The state officials designated 37 programs in the 13 states as meeting that definition.

We wanted to know the major goals of each program, its scope, history, procedures, distinctive aspects, costs, funding sources, and other items. Our interview form contained ten categories, and a total of 32 items. (A sample copy is reproduced on page at right.)

We succeeded in reaching 31 of the program directors in telephone interviews. An assistant director was contacted in one case, and a hotline volunteer responded in still another. Generally the respondents were cooperative, although a few showed reticence in answering the questions of a stranger via telephone. We requested documents and received many.

Notes were taken during each interview, and later revised. A summary description was prepared for each program. Items were coded and responses were tabulated.

Our list of programs encountered in the literature yielded several outstanding programs omitted by the experts in the later, more formal survey. The discrepancies between the lists caused us to doubt the state of awareness of some of our informants.

Surprisingly, of a total of 77 programs identified from the literature and telephone survey, only *four* appeared on *both* lists, which suggests how little information was available at that time, even to sup-

<u>SURVEY</u>

Noteworthy Projects and Programs for Prevention of Drug Abuse

1. Location: _____ _____

                                                Inner-city, suburban, other

2. Who identified project as "noteworthy"?_____

   His comments, if any._____

3. Project name, if any._____

   Sponsoring Agency_____

4. Major Goals (stated in a phrase or two):

5. Scope: _____ _____ _____ _____

         Students (number)   Schools (number)   Grade Levels   Teachers (number)

   _____   _____

   Other staff (number and kind)   Other agencies and groups participating.

6. History: _____ _____ _____ _____

        Date Started.   Short term or continuing?   Still operating?   Expanding?

   _____   _____

          In what respects?   Replication sites, if any.

   _____ _____ _____

     Evaluation attempted?   Evaluation reports available?   Copies ordered.

7. Procedures and stages:

8. What makes project unusual or distinctive?

9. Costs: Estimated Total $_____   Major budget items_____

   _____   Sources of funds (with respective amounts, if known)

10. Survey Respondent_____Title_____

   _____ _____

       Telephone   Address

   Descriptive documents promised?_____

                          Date surveyed   April 1970

                          IED Interviewer_____

                          Code Number_____

posedly well-qualified persons, on the location and characteristics of outstanding drug education programs. It is small wonder that educators report difficulty in finding and learning about schools and communities with valuable experiences in drug education.

Both lists included suburban and city schools in about equal numbers. A strong preference was shown for community-wide and district-wide organization rather than efforts confined to a single school. The latter, in fact, were quite rare. The programs ranged from token projects to highly professional and large-scale endeavors.

Out of 33 programs surveyed, 25 reported that they had not planned an evaluation. Most of these respondents stated or implied that they did not intend to attempt evaluation, largely because of financial or time pressures, as well as the sheer difficulty of measuring results of drug education.

All 33 programs were described by respondents as "long term." None that we could locate had feasible ideas for measuring how far they had come toward meeting their objectives. "Maybe," as Jerry Levine, a drug specialist, suggests, "they will know that they have done a good job when nobody needs them anymore."

The survey led us to the conclusion that very few schools as of early 1970 had broken new ground in developing ways to cope with the drug behavior of the youth culture.

New Insights and Promising Approaches

Many signs of improvement in school drug programs began to appear, however, in the six month interval following our (IED) telephone survey.

An interesting example is provided by peer leadership programs in the Westchester County, New York school systems, including those in Yonkers, Tarrytown, Greenburgh, Port Chester, and Katonah. Launched in the fall of 1970 through encouragement and funding by Lawrence Valenstein, an advertising executive, the programs responded to the theory that students can best motivate their peers. Also, student steering committees selected their faculty advisors instead of the usual procedure.

According to an interview in *The New York Times*, October 26, 1970, Robert Petrillo, drug edu-

cation coordinator for the Greenburgh Central Seven school district, affirms "There's been an overwhelming demand among kids for this kind of peer-to-peer focus."

Sixteen New York City high schools embarked upon similar ventures in 1970 under the assumption that peer pressures are a major factor in drug abuse, and therefore prevention programs under peer leadership might work to offset drug abuse.

The New York City Board of Education was so impressed with the operations and potential of the peer programs during the experimental phase that they expanded the programs the following year. However, the fiscal crisis and political tensions in the city and state with resultant threats of cutbacks for drug education programs, made it difficult to estimate the number of continuing school and community programs. The Board, however, has continued its faculty training for the positions when, and if, they can be financed. The director of peer-group programs for the Board believes that peer groups can work in schools only if there is a full-time faculty member assigned to the group to act as liaison with the school administration and community and as advisor to the students.

Many programs throughout the country have put to use ideas and methods developed in three pioneering ventures described hereafter. Although the effectiveness of these programs has been demonstrated primarily through testimony of participants and other indirect evidence, nevertheless, local convictions as to positive benefits and long-range results are strong.

The three programs are situated in distinct types of communities: a small city in a predominantly agricultural region (Salinas, California); a suburb immediately adjacent to the San Diego metropolitan area (Coronado, California); and an inner-city district of a major urban complex (New York City).

Program in Salinas, California

The Salinas Union High School District took the lead and enlisted the Salinas Police Department, Monterey County Probation Department, Juvenile Hall, Health Department and other public agencies in a cooperative effort to develop a forceful and extensive educational program on drug abuse.

The program includes: inservice training for all teachers, counselors, and administrators; training workshops for juvenile judges, probation officers, juvenile hall supervisors, and public health personnel; counseling with individual students and parents; classroom presentations; and parent education classes. Hundreds of speeches have been given to youth and adult groups of every kind.

In addition, the school district has taken the leadership in developing the Salinas Area Youth Center, a place where young people can go for confidential help in breaking away from dangerous drug use or in avoiding drug involvement without fear of police or other reprisal.

In developing the Salinas approach, the school district consulted many segments of the community as to their feelings concerning drug abuse and as to what role the school should play in dealing with student drug users.

According to one of the written reports on the program, researching the drug problems in the area was vital. "One of the most important aspects of our investigation was our involvement with our students," the report explains. "Students in all schools were consulted. They were given a part in creating their own drug education program by asking them how they felt the program should be approached."

The "philosophy" of the Salinas program is as follows: ". . . the staff has approached the [drug] problem as a symptom of the alienation of youth and the thrust of our effort is directed to working toward the modification or elimination of those aspects of community life which contribute most to this alienation. The structure of the district's program is also designed to deal with the immediate problems of students involved in drug abuse, including crisis situations involving students and their relationship with their parents. While the pharmacology of drugs is of importance as information provided to students, the district holds that providing this information will have little effect in reducing drug abuse."

A teacher was selected to direct the program and, according to Salinas sources, perhaps his most important quality was his complete commitment to the youths he served. He was released from his teaching assignment to devote full time to gaining knowledge related to prevention of drug abuse. Time and funds were provided for him to travel, work, visit, and study the drug scene.

At the high school level, the teacher specialist works with ninth through twelfth graders. In addition, all tenth grade students enrolled in driver education receive an instructional unit on the relationship of drugs and narcotics to driving—this from driver education teachers who have had several hours of inservice training on the drug scene.

Emphasis throughout is on the development of the student's personality and the underlying causes of drug use by youth. The program treats adolescent drug abuse as a symptom of a larger problem: a serious breakdown in communications between adults and young people, which gives rise to many individual and social problems, one of which is adolescent drug abuse. The staff reports that lively and valuable discussions have centered on the topic "Turning on to Life Without Chemicals."

The successes perceived at Salinas seem to be related to powerful insights on the part of the staff. "One of the things we see when we begin to work with students who are drug users is that the drug problem usually drops out of the conversation very quickly," says the above-mentioned report. "The drug is only incidental to the problem. The problem for most students cannot be solved by removing them from school and community. Nor can such problems be dealt with by looking at the failures of the past. We must meet a student at a point of immediate need and try to help him go forward from there. An immediate, nonjudgmental, nonpunitive approach is used and has proven to be extremely satisfactory.

"We are *not* permissive about drug abuse. . . . Teachers and counselors working with our young people try to create a climate in which authentic relationships can develop. We attempt to come together as people, rather than maintain our distance as adults. Trust and authentic relationships can develop only as we risk something of our own personal security with another. There can be no sitting back in the chair with a 'ho-hum' attitude, listening to the plight of the student, helping him to clarify his problem. Teachers and counselors actually participate with the student as he tries to work his way through his problems. The student must be shown positive support—and positive support is not necessarily agreement.

"The teacher needs to seek to understand the problem, not as he sees it, but as the student sees it, and must at all times maintain respect for the integrity of the student whom he is counseling. It is important that the teacher be aware that all students are unique, and that . . . one is careful not to try to solve the problems, but to help the student come to some conclusion about solving the problem himself. . . . It is made clear that all confidences are a sacred trust; this cannot be over-emphasized. . . . The number of referrals being received by the teacher specialists and counselors indicates we are relating to our students and are able to provide a service for them."

It is clear from this that the Salinas staff has deep convictions and that it is convinced that progress is being made.

Program in Coronado, California

This effort began in March, 1968, as an ESEA Title III project entitled "Innovative Program to Solve the Problems of Drug Misuse by Teen and Subteen Cultures." Its ambitious aims and serious research and development aspects make this probably the most complex and far-reaching school drug program in the U.S.

The first stage of the Coronado project was devoted to careful investigation of the local drug situation. Sociologists, cultural anthropologists, and educational and clinical psychologists were retained as consultants to assist the staff in mapping research and development steps. Evaluation was planned at the outset.

Herbert O. Brayer, a high school teacher with experience as a medical association executive, was placed in charge and provided with a full time assistant, Zella Cleary. They were selected, as were other teachers involved, for "previously demonstrated ability to establish rapport" with high school students, according to Supt. Clifford W. Jordan.

During the first stage consultants developed instruments that were used to structure several hundred in-depth interviews conducted with students by the project staff. An important by-product of this preparatory work is the possibility that a predictive instrument, useful in diagnosing individual student propensities toward drug dependency, and perhaps drug misuse, will be developed.

The massive interviewing effort intensified stu-dent involvement and developed into a more or less continuing, informal counseling process. The students embarked upon frank and serious discussions of the project efforts and the kinds of drugs employed by local high school pupils. The project staff made a conscious effort to avoid activities that could be construed as therapy.

The project staff also collected publications dealing with drugs—and acquired, as a result, what is probably the best school collection of materials on that subject in the country. "Look it up!" became the byword that helped to build trust for the project and bind teachers and students together with information and assumptions that both could accept.

In stage two, the project staff set out to analyze how the teenage value structure may be understood and consequently reinforced, influenced, and altered. With the aid of consultants and students, the staff set for itself the staggering task of formulating a broad curriculum related to values and decision-making. The model developed by Mr. Brayer and others is a variation on the Lasswell-Rucker and Carney "systems." It aims to enhance and increase the opportunities and choices of individuals faced with decisions. It attacks antisocial, emotionalized, and superficial attitudes first, and attempts to develop deep and responsible values as a basis for behavior and choice-making—with respect to drug use, as you might expect, but in decision areas as well.

In stage three the plan calls for educationally initiated behavior changes. Pupils may experiment upon volunteer parents in a landmark attempt to change parents' drug habits, at least with respect to tobacco and alcohol.

It is expected that peer relationships will come into play in intensified ways. "We have long recognized," says Superintendent Jordan, "that older high school students exert tremendous pressure and influence upon younger students, including those in the junior high school. We recognize that older high school students are a tremendous influence upon those who are just beginning self-experiments with such drugs as alcohol, tobacco, speed, marijuana, LSD, and the hallucinogens. We hope that, through this program, the weight of that influence will fall within the areas which our generation considers enlightened and that the result will be a step forward for the young people of our community."

Program in New York City

Located at 1300 Boynton Avenue in the Bronx, James Monroe High School serves about 5,000 students enrolled in double sessions. Population shifts in the area alter ethnic distributions in the school from year to year, but usually the student body is composed of black, Spanish-speaking, and white groups in about equal parts.

The drug problem at Monroe, according to some of the teachers, grew quite noticeably more severe a couple of years ago, yet it was probably comparable to the experience suffered by many core-city high schools. Experimentation with heroin, cocaine, mescaline, and marijuana appears to have been common. Medical emergencies arising from overdoses sometimes occurred several times daily.

The program began with appointment of a speech teacher and former dean, Jerry Levine, as full time drug education specialist. Mr. Levine decided to name his office the Drug Information Service, and he set out to gain student participation in the planning and development of a program. That was a key decision. The pattern of full student participation shaped all of the events that followed.

Since Mr. Levine was well known to many students—and trusted and respected by them—his new office in the basement (near the furnace) attracted attention and interest. Every day additional students came to inquire and to discuss drugs informally. The students formed the Brotherhood Establishment for the purpose of discouraging drug abuse. Strict behavioral rules requiring avoidance of drugs and mutual assistance were adopted, and within a week or so the Brotherhood's ranks had increased to 60 students.

Meanwhile, Mr. Levine quietly explained the students' program to interested faculty members. Soon faculty volunteers were taking part in the more-or-less nonstop group counseling sessions in his small office. Smoking was permitted, despite strong reservations on the part of the school administration. Mr. Levine broke dress regulations by appearing regularly without tie and jacket, and finally, despite official disapproval, he appeared at school in blue jeans.

In effect the students created not so much a program as a counterculture. The new culture treats drugs as "un-cool." It appears highly probable that only the students could have accomplished this. The Brotherhood membership cuts across all lines including ethnic, age and sex classifications, and includes former users and some who have never touched drugs.

Within a few weeks between 150 and 200 students *per day* were coming in to the Drug Information Service for literature, group counseling or personal assistance. The Brotherhood accepted 71 members, weeded out a few, and now has a deeply motivated round-the-clock group of workers. Influence has spread from school to neighborhood; and during the summer 36 students worked against drugs as volunteers at the San Juan Center (social services and medical), in addition to working at the school. Five were employed as teacher aides in the Monroe summer program, and several more in each of two new storefront community centers.

There are ten student-speaker teams, usually coed, all of whom have conducted classes, some of them numerous times, with faculty sponsorship.

Over 50 Monroe teachers have volunteered to help in the program, 20 of whom have been regularly attending weekly attitudinal and skills training sessions, without compensation.

As the risks in student leadership began to be reduced by demonstrated acceptance of responsibility, the Monroe administration met the program more than halfway, and in the last months of the spring term gave full support to both student and faculty leadership.

The Faculty Drug Specialist: A Key Person

There are so few outstanding programs of drug abuse education, . . . that it is difficult to generalize about effective approaches. One fact is clear, however; it stands out in the findings of our survey and in the reports presented above: the most important element of an effective program is a full-time staff specialist appointed as coordinator of drug education or, preferably, director of drug information services—a nonauthoritarian title that speaks to student and teacher demand for reliable information on subjects related to drugs.

One of the important duties of this specialist should be the assembly and management of an information library for students and faculty. He can also find and screen outside resources that might be helpful to drug education in the school. He can advise administration and staff on drug problems and maintain liaison with other agencies interested in prevention of drug abuse. Also, he should bring leadership to workshops and actually conduct in-service training. He should be the prime resource of the school and the district in explaining the drug education program to parents and community groups, and should be prepared to accept speaking engagements and serve on civic committees.

The highest priority in allocation of his time, however, should go to direct contacts with students. A full-time staff specialist can be quite effective in helping high school students with organization of their own prevention projects, in building bridges of trust between the youth subculture and the faculty, and in counseling individuals and small groups of students. . . .

Donald E. Barnes in "The Drug Problem: New Insights and Promising Approaches" from High School Principal's Service, *Operational Briefing.* **Croft Educational Services Inc., Nov., 1970.**

What interests us most about the Monroe High School drug program is the fact that it happened in much the way we had imagined. A school selected the right kind of teacher and then supported him in his efforts to carry out a radically new kind of approach to students in trouble with drugs. The following selections give an indication of what can happen when students are provided with space, time, and the right catalyst—in this case a former speech teacher.

During the summer of 1970 the Community News Service (CNS) ran five stories about the Monroe program, the first of which we reprint in full.

May 14, 1970 (CNS)—The drug problem at James Monroe High School, on Boynton Avenue in the Bronx, is probably no worse than in many other city high schools. According to teachers involved in trying to solve that problem, at least one student each day requires treatment for drug use: on Tuesday, a student was taken to the hospital after an overdose of cocaine; the day before there were two "OD" cases, one involving pills.

The difference is that at Monroe a group of students and a small nucleus of teachers are working to do something more about drugs than get student users arrested. The Board of Education and a business group are also lending a hand.

At the beginning of the second semester, a Monroe teacher and former school dean, Jerry Levine, was appointed as Monroe's Drug Information Service (DIS) Officer under a Board of Education program that hopefully will be extended to all city high schools next fall. He and a teacher at Brandeis High School are the first in the city.

The DIS program which Levine is running was designed primarily by the students and Levine feels that this is the major reason that it appears to be working so well.

The cooperative effort started about four months ago with a few students who were helping each other kick their habits. Calling itself The Brotherhood Establishment, the group soon expanded to include many students less personally involved, but equally concerned about drugs at Monroe. Membership cuts across all lines, and includes Blacks, Puerto Ricans and Whites, about 60 in all.

While some of the members used to be "on everything" including heroin, some have never touched drugs. "We wanted to deal with the drug problem in the school, and we decided the best way to do it was through the students," said 19-year-old Conrad Villar, Jr., a student at Monroe, and president of The Brotherhood Establishment.

The DIS program at Monroe, Levine said, is founded on three "working philosophies".

1. Since kids turn each other on, they are the best source to turn each other off;

2. A counter-culture has to be created that regards drugs as 'un-cool';

3. The participants must gain a sense of dignity and pride by having meaningful responsibilities to carry out.

Levine points out that Temple University did a long and expensive study on drug use in high schools, and came out with recommendations exactly like the program that the Brotherhood outlined in a few hours of conversation with him.

Levine's salary comes from the Board of Education, and money for materials is supplied by the Economic Development Council's Partnership Project at the school. The EDC, composed of some 90 major businesses in New York, has two partnership projects with city high schools, and supplies funds for special programs in those schools. It is assisted by the Institute for Educational Development.

One of the DIS projects—all of which are run primarily by the Brotherhood with Levine's advice and assistance—is dealing with drug crises in the school. When a student "OD's" in school, a Brotherhood "crisis" team goes to work to find out what that student was taking, so that the hospital can swiftly give him the appropriate treatment.

If a teacher suspects that one of her students is on drugs, she sends his name in a sealed envelope to Levine, who refers it to the Brotherhood team on duty. The team then checks the kid out. If he is a user, they try to talk him out of drugs, and tell him of the help available from the DIS. If he is not a user, the teacher is informed of the mistake.

"One disadvantage of our education program is over-reaction by some of the teachers," says Levine. "Sometimes a kid is just tired, and the teacher is convinced he is 'nodding.'"

Teams of Brotherhood members are also available for any teacher to invite into a subject class. When the team comes to speak in a class, the teacher leaves the room and the door is closed, so that the students can talk with the team without fear of exposure.

"The biggest stumbling block to therapy for the kids is the parents," Levine asserts, "because they still feel that going for therapy is admitting the problem exists and that it is a negative reflection on them." Other problems exist because parents are ignorant of the jargon and paraphernalia of drugs.

To educate parents, Levine organized a series of four seminars. At the first seminar held May 12, 1970, the parents filed into a room saturated with a marijuana-like odor, produced by burning pellets designed to simulate pot. Few of the parents could identify the odor; some guessed incense.

When Marlene Walters, a physical education teacher at Monroe who has been working with Levine on the drug project, suggested that the odor could be covered by spraying room deodorizer, many of the parents recalled that their children often sprayed room deodorizer at home. The point was not lost on the parents.

For the next few hours, the parents listened as Miss Walters and students from the Brotherhood ran through the basics of drug jargon and equipment. The parents asked many detailed questions about drug use, and the students and Miss Walters supplied the answers.

As one student puts it, "It was like a rap ses-sion, but you'd never see a rap session like that between parents and their own kids."

"The only way to fight the drug problem," Levine said, "is to create a vanguard of highly-motivated, well-trained people. We already have a vanguard of 200 participating kids and teachers, and now we need to get into the community."

To bring the program into the community, the Brotherhood Establishment obtained an office for the summer, a basement, at 1715 Bryant Avenue.

The Economic Development Council and the Board of Education agreed to fund the summer program at the school.

From Community News Service, Inc., New York, N. Y.

We remain in close touch with the Brotherhood Establishment. There have been many changes in organization as the students have discovered their strengths and limitations. For instance, during one stage of their growth, which they now refer to as the "ego trip," there were about 20 officers of the Brotherhood, and now in 1972 there are two. They decided to limit membership to a hardworking cadre not to exceed 60 members, with new members going through a probationary period, during which they must keep certain commitments and meet certain conditions before they become eligible. All members are required to take training in group processes, leadership, awareness, public speaking, etc., and if they are not given assignments, they are told to think up projects. "Don't just stand there, rexograph something."

By the end of the second school year the Brotherhood had sweated out a weekly newspaper, a music and poetry project, a book in first draft, and an information service based on everything you can do and get free in the city. Two former members opened a boutique across the street from the school. The summer project evolved for the second year was a six-week summer school emphasizing career preparation and choice.

The group raises its own funds, and carries its message to other schools and into the community through its speaker teams, and through posters and flyers distributed throughout the community.

During March, 1971, James Monroe High adjourned classes for two days for teachers to attend a seminar conducted by the Brotherhood. Although the students had participated in weekly rap sessions with volunteer teachers who have joined in their efforts, this was their first attempt to "teach teachers."

Max E. Ostrover, Acting Principal at James Monroe High School, in a letter to Mr. Levine said, "The program . . . involving the teachers and pupils in narcotic seminars seems to have been a resounding success." Mr. Ostrover further stated the desire to follow up the meetings with some concrete results and congratulated Mr. Levine and members of the Brotherhood for a job well done.

The following guidelines contain a list of suggestions that may be used for the creation of a student-centered drug prevention program. Students are reminded that this does not provide all of the answers, and that it is by no means the only way to do it. It is intended to stimulate thinking and to show how one program is working at this time.

I. Select a leader from among yourselves. This must be someone who is respected, reliable, willing to learn and listen to others, and capable of devoting long hours of hard work. He or she need not be a former drug abuser. A person who can relate to and communicate well with others will be able to deal with drug abusers. It is the abuser who does not relate well.

II. Choose an adult advisor who gets along well with people your age, is sincere, dedicated, and able to work with people on both sides of the fence. He should be able to help you find and tap resources, be aware of your rights, and be able to help you develop your potential. But don't ask him to provide all the answers.

III. Develop a core group of people your age who will listen, think, and do things. This group along with the leader and advisor, will be the backbone of the organization. Establish a realistic set of goals and rules of discipline and stick by them. You will lead by example. The Brotherhood Establishment was started by two students and myself.

IV. Get a place to work. You need an office that offers privacy and a ready availability. This will be your base of operations. If you can't get the following items, find out where there are people who will let you use a typewriter, a duplicating machine (a rexograph is fine), supplies, and some shelves. You must get your own phone. You are going to have to guarantee that all conversations are held in the strictest confidence.

V. Work yourselves to the bone getting as much drug information as is possible. Get the real facts and train yourselves. Find out about the different ways to handle the problem. Include prevention, rehabilitation, and the laws dealing with drugs.

VI. Start a referral system. Know where to send people who want treatment. Know what to do if you come across someone who has taken an overdose. Make a working list of all treatment centers in your area. Let those people know you are there.

VII. Decide what you think you are able to do. Then publicize yourselves to let everyone know who you are, what you stand for, and what you are ready to do. Make your office available as a "rap" room. See that it is staffed, with your members ready to talk, listen, and give out information and help. If you want to stay in business, never abuse the confidence and trust that people will place in you.

VIII. When recruiting try to be selective, and let people know that you are. Your progress will depend upon how willingly and how well you all work together. Don't let just anyone in. It is crucial that you do not permit "dead weight" to stay in the group.

IX. Never stop training and learning. Teach each other and develop your potentials. Part of your development will be solving problems that exist among yourselves. If you can't solve your own, then the chances are that you can't solve anyone else's either.

X. Understand that you will be disappointed on occasion, but also that you will, if you really work, save lives and keep families together. Understand that this is one of the toughest problems to lick and that every time you fall you must get up again and keep going. Learn from your mistakes, and know that people like us are doing well when there is no longer a need for what we're doing.

Jerry Levine's guidelines from the weekly, *Scholastic Voice*, March 8, 1971.

More Peer Group Programs

There is great variety in peer-group programs. One of the largest is known as DOPE STOP Teen Involvement, in Maricopa County, Arizona, which has more than 1,600 high school students enrolled as Teen Counselors for grades 5-8. The program started in 1969 as a project of the Maricopa Mental Health Association, and was funded by the State of Arizona, the County Board of Supervisors and several cities in Maricopa County.

DOPE STOP places importance on the fact that the Teen Counselors do not use drugs. Though they have had opportunities to do so, they explain to the younger students that they have made a decision. As Gladys E. Conroy, former Director of DOPE STOP, puts it, "If the decision has been made in advance, the child is prepared for that moment. Indeed far more young people are strung out on drugs today who did not make a decision about drugs than those who did."

The ongoing Teen Involvement program is presented to approximately 30,000 elementary school students each month through visits from the Teen Counselors. The selection of Teen Counselors is made by the high school administration from a list of volunteers. Strict requirements include that the student counselor not be a drug user, and is sincere in his efforts to put time into learning and spreading the information on drugs. Although the vast majority of the Teen Counselors have never been involved with drugs, some former users have also participated.

In addition to the 30,000 elementary students exposed to the program monthly, DOPE STOP, through its speakers' bureau, reaches between 2,000 to 5,000 persons weekly through presentations to schools, service clubs, churches, business groups, etc. DOPE STOP also assists the State Department of Public Instruction by providing in-service training for educators.

One of the high school students who supervised a group of Teen Counselors in his senior year became a fulltime employee as coordinator of counselors the following year. He makes monthly visits to each high school throughout the county, acting as a resource person for Teen Counselors who bring back from the grade schools questions they were unable to answer. Teen Counselors are urged to hold monthly meetings to exchange new ideas and information. They are trained to say "I don't know" when a question comes up they cannot answer, and not to rely on bluffing or guesswork.

We have not yet found a peer-group program confined to students of elementary school ages, though we dare say such programs are on the way, judging by the emphasis on values and decision-making we have encountered in numerous K-6 curricula we have reviewed. The introduction to the Grades K-3 curricula on drug abuse education, developed by the South Bay Union School District, Imperial Beach, California, concludes:

"We live in a society which provides limitless opportunity for children to discover and become informed about any and all topics and we must never underestimate the potency of the peer group as a teacher. As adults, both parents and teachers, we must learn to respond to youth's discovery of the world and their perception of it (which may differ from ours) with candor and acceptance of their desires and abilities to participate in meaningful social decisions. . . . Perhaps our deepest concern at this time should be to help our young people develop effective concepts about themselves and positive feelings about our society rather than devising more elaborate and repressive outside controls on their behavior which we can neither justify nor enforce."

Community Involvement

A walk-in, free clinic for people on drugs, including addicts, attempts to deal with some of the ugliest and most forlorn aspects of life in America. It makes a direct approach to human need that often cannot be made by other medical institutions or by other groups or agencies in society.

Since the Haight-Ashbury Clinic in California was founded in 1967, more than 200 other free clinics have opened in all parts of the country. In California alone, 45 free clinics report that they see an average of 31,000 patients a month, with the Haight-Ashbury Clinic accounting for nearly 5,000 a month. It is estimated that nationally the free clinics handle two million patient visits a year, and that 600,000 Americans are now receiving some kind of health care from these alternative institutions. Dr. David E. Smith, pioneer of the free clinic movement, is President of the National Free Clinic Council, which held its second annual symposium in Washington, D.C., January, 1972.

According to evidence reported in the press, these informal outpatient facilities are a prime means of recovering many of the people who are not yet addicted.

. . . Many of the young people who hang out on Haight Street are not only overtly or potentially psychotic, but also physically ravaged by one another as well. Although murder is not particularly popular with the new population, some of its members seem to spend their lives in plaster casts. Others frequently exhibit suppurating abrasions, knife and razor slashes, damaged genitalia and other types of traumatic injuries—injuries all caused by violence.

Even more visible is the violence they do to themselves. Continually stoned on drugs, the adolescents often over-exert and fail to notice as they infect and mangle their feet by wading through the droppings and broken glass. Furthermore, although some of the heroin addicts lead a comparatively stabilized existence, others overlook the physiological deterioration which results from their self-destructive lives. The eating habits of these young people are so poor that they are often malnourished and inordinately susceptible to infectious disease. In fact, a few of them suffer from protein and vitamin deficiencies that are usually found only in chronic alcoholics three times their age.

With gums bleeding from pyorrhea and rotting teeth, some also have abscesses and a diffuse tissue infection called cellulitis, both caused by using dirty needles. Others miss their veins while shooting up or rupture them by injecting impure and undissolvable chemicals. And since most sleep, take drugs and have sex in unsanitary environments, they constantly expose themselves to upper respiratory tract infections, skin rashes, bronchitis, tonsillitis, influenza, dysentery, urinary and genital tract infections, hepatitis and venereal disease.

In addition to these and other chronic illnesses, the young people also suffer from a wide range of drug problems. Some have acute difficulties, such as those individuals who oversedate themselves with barbiturates or "overamp" with amphetamines. Others have chronic complaints, long-term "speed"-precipitated psychoses and paranoid, schizophrenic reactions. Many require physiological and psychological withdrawal from barbiturates and heroin. In fact, heroin addiction and its attendant symptoms have reached epidemic proportions in the Haight-Ashbury, and the few doctors at Park Emergency Hospital cannot check the spread of disease and drug abuse through the district any better than the police can control its crime.

To make matters worse, these physicians appear unwilling to attempt to solve the local health problems. Like many policemen, the public health representatives seem to look on young drug-abusers as subhuman. When adolescents come to Park Emergency for help the doctors frequently assault them with sermons, report them to the police or submit them to complicated and drawn-out referral procedures that only intensify their agony. The nurses sometimes tell prospective patients to take their problems elsewhere. The ambulance drivers simply "forget" calls for emergency assistance. They and the other staff members apparently believe that the best way to stamp out sickness in the Haight is to let its younger residents destroy themselves.

Given this attitude, it is hardly surprising that the adolescents are as frightened of public health officials as they are of policemen. Some would sooner risk death than seek aid at Park Emergency and are equally unwilling to go to San Francisco General Hospital, the city's central receiving unit, two miles away. Many merely live with their symptoms, doctor themselves with home remedies or narcotize themselves to relieve their pain. These young people do not trust "straight" private physicians, who they assume will overcharge them and hand them over to the law. Uneducated about medical matters, they too often listen only to the "witch doctors" and drug-dealers who prowl the Haight-Ashbury, prescribing their own products for practically every physiological and psychological ill.

A few are receptive to responsible opinion and anxious to be properly treated, particularly those individuals who want to kick heroin and those younger adolescents who have just made the Haight their home. Unfortunately, however, they have nowhere to go for help. . . .

The Clinic: An Alternative

. . . although it is still somewhat at odds with the local medical Establishment, the clinic is better staffed and funded than at any point in its 2½-year history. It is also more decentralized, with several facilities in and outside of the Haight-Ashbury. Its oldest operation, a Medical Section located on the second floor of a faded yellow building at the corner of Haight and Clayton Streets, is now open from six until ten five evenings a week. Over 40 dedicated volunteers are on hand in the 14-room former dentist's office, so that 558 Clayton Street can accommodate more than 50 patients a day. . . .

Whatever their motivation, the doctors' primary objectives are diagnosis and detoxification. After examining their patients, they attempt to treat some with donated drugs which are kept under lock and key in the clinic pharmacy. Others require blood, urine and vaginal smear tests that can be performed in the laboratory on equipment furnished by the Medical Logistics Company of San Francisco and its 35-year-old president, Donald Reddick, who serves as the clinic's administrative director. Most of the patients have chronic problems, however, and cannot be treated adequately on the premises. They must therefore be referred and/or physically transported to other facilities, such as Planned Parenthood, the Society for Humane Abortions, the Pediatrics Clinic at the University of California Medical Center on Parnassus Street six blocks south, Children's Hospital, San Francisco General Hospital and the Public Health Department Clinic for VD. The Medical Section maintains a close working relationship with these institutions and can therefore act as a buffer between its hip patients and the straight world.

Although the physicians and nurses contribute to this mediating process, much of the referring, chauffeuring and patient-contacting at 558 Clayton Street is carried out by its staff of clerks, administrative aides and paramedical volunteers. Twenty such young people donate their time and energy to the Medical Section at present, most of them student activists, conscientious objectors fulfilling alternative service requirements and former members of the Haight-Ashbury's new community. Emotionally equipped to handle the demands and the depressing climate of ghetto medicine, several core members of the paramedical staff live together in the Haight as a communal family. . . .

Since heroin addiction is such a pressing current problem, Dr. Matzger and an anesthesiologist named Dr. George Gay have recently launched a heroin withdrawal program at the Medical Section.

Working there five afternoons a week for the past four months, the two physicians have treated over 200 patients, less than 50 percent of whom consider the Haight their home. "The remainder are adolescents from so-called good families," Dr. Matzger reports, "most of them students at local colleges and high schools. Significantly, they follow the same evolutionary pattern as young people have in this district, progressing from hallucinogenic drug abuse to abuse of amphetamines and then to abuse of barbiturates and opiates. The 'Year of the Middle-Class Junkie' in San Francisco may well be 1970. If it is, we hope to extend our program as addiction problems mount throughout the entire Bay area." . . .

On the third floor at 409 Clayton Street is the clinic publications office, staffed by volunteers who oversee the preparation of *The Journal of Psychedelic Drugs*, a semi-annual compilation of articles and papers presented at the drug symposia sponsored by the clinic and the University of California Medical Center Psychopharmacology Study Group. Aided by several health professionals, the volunteers also answer requests for medical information and administer the affairs of the National Free Clinics Council, an organization created in 1968 for the dozens of free facilities in Berkeley, Boston, and other cities that modeled their efforts after those of the Haight-Ashbury Free Medical Clinic programs.

Sandwiched in between the Publications Office and Reverend Grosjean's sanctuary is the Psychiatric Section. This service, which is supervised by Stuart Loomis, a 47-year-old associate professor of education at San Francisco State College, provides free counseling and psychiatric aid for over 150 individuals. Roughly one-half of these patients are hippies and "active hippies" who either live in the district or commute from rural and urban communes where physicians from the Medical Section make house calls. The remaining 50 percent is made up of young people who suffer from the chronic anxiety and depression common in heroin addicts.

Loomis and the other 30 staff psychologists, psychiatrists and psychiatric social workers at 409 Clayton Street are able to counsel some of these patients in the Psychiatric Section. They usually refer the more disturbed multiple drug-abusers and ambulatory schizophrenics now common to the

Haight either to such facilities as the drug program at Mendocino State Hospital or to the Immediate Psychiatric Aid and Referral Service at San Francisco General, whose director, Dr. Arthur Carfagni, is on the clinic's executive committee. When intensive psychiatric intervention is not called for, however, they frequently send the patients to the clinic's own Drug Treatment Program in the basement downstairs.

Project "Free Fuse"

This project, nicknamed the Free Fuse, is led by a Lutheran minister in his mid-thirties named John Frykman. Financed by personal gifts and by grants from such private foundations as the Merrill Trust, its goal is to wean drug-abusers away from their destructive life-style. Using methods developed by Synanon and the Esalen Institute, Frykman and the other Free Fuse counselors have attempted to create a close and productive social unit out of alienated adolescents living together as the clinic's second communal family. They have also provided educational and employment opportunities for more than 500 young people in the past 1½ years.

Since many Free Fuse graduates are still involved in his project, Frykman has also found it possible to expand. Having recently opened an annex in the drug-ridden North Beach District under the supervision of a psychiatric nurse, he has allowed the Drug Treatment Program to geographically qualify for inclusion in the Northeast Mental Health Center, a cachement area encompassing one-quarter of San Francisco. Because of this, the Free Fuse will participate in a substantial grant from the National Institute of Mental Health being administered by Dr. Carfagni. Frykman's Drug Treatment Program has already received some of these funds, and he is therefore making arrangements with the downtown YMCA to open a similar center in the city's Tenderloin area. "We've never gotten a penny from any public agency before," he says, "but the future looks bright from here."

This optimism certainly seems justified, and Frykman is not the only staff member who insists that the clinic is in better shape than at any other point in its history. Yet, as indicated earlier, the facility has problems all the same. In the first place, although the volunteers working at 409 and 558 Clayton Street can point to their share of therapeutic successes, they cannot really help most of the individuals who now live in the Haight-Ashbury. Many of the volunteers are actually former patients; some of them can keep off drugs only if they are kept on the staff.

Second, and most important, is the fact that the Haight continues to deteriorate in spite of the clinic's efforts. Thus, the relatively healthy adolescents tend to abandon the district, leaving behind their more disturbed counterparts, as well as the older individuals who preceded them in the area. Because of this, some staff members at the Medical and Psychological Sections believe that the clinic has outlived its usefulness in its present form. Others argue that the facility should address itself to the problems not only of the new population but of the old community as well . . . for the clinic's future, like its past, is intimately connected with the district it serves.

David E. Smith, John Luce and Ernest A. Dernburg in "The Health of Haight-Ashbury," from *Trans-Action*, April, 1970.

Since the publication of the above article, there have been many changes and expansions of the Haight-Ashbury Free Medical Clinic. The Medical section, as of early 1972, is at 558 Clayton St.; the Drug Treatment section at 529 Clayton; Psychiatric section, 409 Clayton; and publications, 701 Irving, San Francisco, California. *The Journal of Psychedelic Drugs* is published cooperatively by the Haight-Ashbury Free Medical Clinic and the Student Association for the Study of Hallucinogens (STASH), Beloit, Wisconsin.

One of the services an alert community can provide is a hotline, manned by professional and lay volunteers who can give around-the-clock aid to problems telephoned to the nerve center.

More often than not, emergencies related to drugs do not occur during school hours, and the secretive character of experiments with drugs very often demands anonymity. Hence, the telephone line opens up a consulting channel that can save lives under emergency conditions, and that can serve confessional purposes, deal with ignorance and fear, and lend moral courage.

Hotlines are now in operation in many communities. They require training, patience, and a sense of mission for those who man the phones.

Perhaps it would be worth it to some communities to consider the use of skilled and specialized persons to help bring about better communications, according to the following suggestion from the Committee for Psychedelic Drug Information, which amounts to a job description for a communications catalyst.

"Important things that need to be done in the area of community education include the following: Having individuals who are knowledgeable concerning current attitudes and sentiments of youth and also able to understand the problems and perspectives of the adult generation act as communications catalysts in the community by 1) communicating with key persons in a community, school officials, the police chief, city council members, prominent doctors and other professionals, heads of community agencies, persons in hospital administration, psychiatric clinic personnel, etc.; 2) communicating with large organized groups, presenting programs which would be designed to give adults a perspective into the problem of drug abuse and some insight into what might be the most fruitful and the most appropriate courses of action; 3) presenting conferences open to the community in which problems and directions would be discussed; 4) providing for an evening school series which would be directed toward the problem of drug abuse and more importantly, the deeply rooted causes which are leading to it. . . .

Essentially what is being proposed is that persons qualified to act as communications catalysts be employed to work within communities in an effort to deepen community-wide understanding of the problems underlying drug abuse and to stimulate community interest in working to satisfy needs which are currently going unsatisfied."

From the Committee for Psychedelic Drug Information.

It has been said that society gets the drug or disease it needs. Or deserves. There have been arguments that drugs will not go away until the problems of the cities are solved. It is also argued that drugs will plague us as long as youth is marginal to our economic life, as long as youth is trained to consumership, instead of production. Sol Yurick, in "The Political Economy of Junk" takes an unsentimental view of heroin as a necessary evil to society.

. . . How then, to prevent the fabric of society from becoming completely unraveled, does one achieve a reintegration of confidence, a restoration of the faith to fight off internal threats to economic and ideological world goals? How does one re-translate what is a failure of confidence in one mode of productive activity into confidence in a new mode of economic behavior, achieving, at the same time, a tractable labor force, still permitting the rising-expectations syndrome to find outlets for enterprise on the part of those growingly vast segments of the population who are, for all practical purposes, irrelevant?

How does one allow for the rise of new elites whose energies might otherwise be destructive if frustrated?

What product, or set of products, what set of economic relations tends, more than others at this particular time in history, to foster those aims and further the historical development of capitalism, proving to the world its fecund viability?

Only the imaginative use of drugs—especially heroin—fulfills these conditions which call for a vast acceleration of what only the most conservative would call the *illegal* labor force.

Mr. Yurick, an acknowledged Marxist critic, goes on to explain that the illegal labor force is part of our economic system.

. . . Heightened illegal activity is both a response to an expanding economy and a mode of keeping options open for the creation of new capital and new capitalists. The rise in drug consumption is better understood if we regard the matter as a political and economic subsystem contiguous with the rest of the social economy; it is a model of imperfect competition and uneven development, *laissez faire* on the bottom and monopolistic on the top. The junkie's hand is not so much raised against society; rather he is involved in on-the-job training in a true street academy; certainly, for the ghetto dweller, pushing, purchasing, and habit-resolution (the fix) may be his salvation, redeeming him for the market and thus society.

. . . The junkie is a veritable heroic Stakhanovite worker, almost pure economic man, living for the fix, the hunt, the fix, keeping his body alive merely to consume heroin at a rising rate, at the same time circulating enormous quantities of money, retaining only the modest interest of the fix which constantly diminishes (a sort of compound dis-interest) as his habit grows and the product continues to be adulterated. . . . It is in the nature of a high-velocity, high-pressure business cycle that it demands total attention to that business alone. All previous relations that get in the way of 'getting and spending' cycle drop off: family loyalty, sexual feelings, love, cohort loyalty, friendship, brotherhood, compassion. The junkie will be driven to use any means necessary to get the money to buy the product. There's nothing like heroin consumption to teach the real meaning of the work ethic. It is on the junkie's back that a vast economic edifice is being built, one which resolves many economic and political difficulties.

Sol Yurick in article, "The Political Economy of Junk" from *Monthly Review*, **December, 1970.**

Mr. Yurick's article provides a long list of the kinds of people and institutions with a vested interest in the heroin problem. However much one may wish to disagree with Yurick's thesis, there remains the stubborn reality that there are many people with political and economic investments in the drug economy and the power arrangements related to drugs.

Yet in New York City, reputed to be the heroin capital of the world, some reassuring observations come from two high school principals, both of whom acknowledged serious heroin problems among their students in the school year 1969-1970. A year later they reported that for some reason, hopefully but not necessarily associated with aggressive anti-drug programs in their schools, the use of heroin by students had quite evidently slackened. It is quite possible, of course, that the drug cultures will wear themselves out somehow and that replacements perhaps unimagined will appear. That would probably mean a turn for the better, perhaps much better, for the only activities that could rival narcotics addiction in sheer harmfulness would be mass suicides.

Health departments of schools and college campuses troubled with bad trips from acid and overdoses of speed have also reported a tapering-off, suggesting that young people are deciding against certain drugs that they have found, in the long run, not to be worth the trip.

Certain aspects of the powerful rock music phenomenon, notably live concerts for mass audiences, appear to be rolling into oblivion, and with them may go some of the styles in drug consumption and certain myths concerning the ways to peak experiences and the good life via drugs. It seems quite possible that the intensely moral concerns of young people in the current generation may lead them not only away from the drug experience of the '60's but also toward excesses of rectitude in trying to live up to values they seem to be working out for themselves. Scratch a pot-smoker and you may find a vegetarian, a conservationist, gardener, healer,

teacher, lover, poet, contemplative, artisan. Even a dedicated manual laborer. Certainly a pacifist, and a person concerned about mankind's condition.

Meanwhile, what of the professional educators, parents, and others who hold power in their communities and, for the time being, bear society's responsibility for defending itself against unhealthy activities? Few of them are do-nothings, because their sense of passing generations and elapsing time will not permit them to wait for the day when drug cultures may have moved through a cycle and subsided. Every hour counts and every child. For that matter, every ill and endangered human being is a cause for action.

In these pages we have tried to assemble what seemed to us the best lay and technical knowledge on lines of action for helping those who seem unable to help themselves. Everywhere we looked for wisdom and information to pass along, we kept stumbling against a hard yet interesting paradox. Those who hold power in the society are generally the ones raising the most clamor that something must be done about drugs right way; and yet the counsel offered to those who hold power is to share it. And those who would share should begin with listening, seeking to understand those who resist their solicitude, and acknowledging the futility of exercise of power in accustomed ways.

It is even harder to realize, and to act on the realization, that personal example is pivotal in our attempts to overcome something as unwise and evidently self-destructive as drug abuse.

Since so much of man's experience with drugs dates far back, we should not be surprised that some of the best suggestions on what to do about drugs have an ancient ring and overtones of old thoughts on what makes a good man and a good life.

. . . Acknowledging the need for identifying objectives for drug abuse education programs and for the development of techniques for evaluating them, the steering committee of the Education Commission of the States in November, 1970, recommended that the ECS staff analyze state evaluation programs now in effect and determine whether an evaluation model for all states and the nation can be found or developed. If it is deemed necessary, the staff has been authorized to secure funding and proceed with development of an evaluation mechanism for drug abuse education programs.

DRUG EDUCATION FOR TEACHERS

In an effort to determine if teacher training institutions are incorporating drug abuse education into their programs for prospective teachers, the Education Commission of the States during November 1970, in cooperation with the American Association of Colleges of Teacher Education (AACTE), surveyed AACTE member institutions.

Replies have been received from 567 of 840 institutions queried. The results below indicate that well over half of those responding are making some attempt to incorporate drug abuse education into their programs. In those institutions that offer drug abuse education as part of other course offerings, about sixty percent are offered through health education and health and physical education programs. Fourteen percent are offered through education and ten percent through psychology courses. Others mentioned were sociology, law enforcement and biology. Two respondents emphasized that efforts were being made to integrate drug abuse education into all courses. In most cases funding for programs comes directly from departmental or regular college budgets. Minnesota colleges indicated that in order to be certified to teach in that state, prospective teachers must have had some instruction in drug abuse education.

Drug Abuse Education Offered:
    as part of other courses, required 65
    as part of other courses, not required 66
    specific course, required 15
    specific course, not required 51
    through summer institutes, workshops, etc. . . 67

Drug Abuse Education Not Offered:
    no course offered, none planned 184
    inclusion of course being studied 30
    course to be introduced, 1971-1972 49

DRUG ABUSE EDUCATION ACT OF 1970

A major breakthrough in education about the dangers of drug use has been scored with the passage of the Drug Abuse Education Act of 1970. The measure, which authorizes $58 million to be spent over the next three years, was signed by President Nixon December 3. The legislation differs significantly from the Comprehensive Drug Abuse Prevention and Control Act signed by President Nixon on October 27, which stresses law enforcement and rehabilitation. The Drug Abuse Education Act channels funds for drug education programs through the U.S. Office of Education, while the Comprehensive Drug Abuse Prevention and Control Act assigns the authority for its programs to the National Institute of Mental Health.

Approximately $1.45 million of the funds authorized by the new legislation would go directly to state departments of education to help them plan and carry out drug abuse education programs. The bill would authorize $5 million for the fiscal year (1971), $10 million for fiscal 1972, and $14 million for fiscal 1973, for a variety of programs with emphasis on drug education curricula. It would allow the Secretary of Health, Education, and Welfare to make grants and contracts with institutions of higher education, state and local educational agencies, and other public and private research institutions to support research, demonstration, and pilot projects such as the development of new and improved curricular materials for use in elementary, secondary, adult, and community education programs. The measure also calls for preservice and inservice training programs, including seminars, workshops, and conferences on drug abuse education.

An additional $29 million to be spread over a three-year period was added in the Senate for community and adult education on drug abuse. Sen. Edward M. Kennedy (D-Mass.) sponsored this amendment which also includes funds for peer-group programs such as drop-in centers, outpatient counseling, and telephone services to handle calls from youngsters with drug problems. The legislation includes explicit provisions to recruit, train, organize and employ professionals, former drug users, and paraprofessionals to participate in drug education programs. Such provisions were not included in the Comprehensive Drug Abuse Prevention and Control Act.

There is a serious lack of teachers and counselors to provide instruction on the dangers of drug abuse, concludes a House Education and Labor Committee report. It adds that the nation's schools generally are ill equipped to provide objective, scientifically valid instruction on drug use and abuse. The purpose of the Drug Abuse Education Act, the report states, is to "help eliminate drug abuse by striking at the heart of the problem—the lack of knowledge on the part of the average citizen, young or old, on the dangers of improper drug use."

From *Education, U.S.A.*, Nov. 30, 1970. Copyright 1970, National School Public Relations Association.

STATE BY STATE SURVEY

Alabama—As a follow-up on the Governor's Statewide Conference in February of 1970 on drug education, the Alabama State Department of Education has established a team of six educational specialists in drug education. The state drug abuse team is holding workshops statewide attended by teachers, students and interested laymen. The team also accepts invitations from colleges and universities, civic clubs and any interested lay group that is concerned with the critical problem of drug abuse. This effort is funded under the Education Professions Development Act (EPDA). Contact: William A. Heustess, Coordinator, State Drug Abuse Education Program, State Department of Education, Montgomery 36104.

The State Board of Health, Division of Narcotics and Dangerous Drugs, is compiling information on drug abuse intensity at the professional level. Legislation is expected to be introduced to insure inclusion of drug abuse education in grades one through twelve, inservice training for teachers, and expansion of degree programs for preparation of drug education specialists, particularly at the junior college level.

Alaska—Governor Keith Miller has appointed a statewide coordinator of drug abuse education in his office to communicate with and unify the aims and goals of community action groups throughout Alaska. The coordinator will help establish guidelines and curricula for the state's education program, legislative goals and special preventive and rehabilitative programs. A team of six from Alaska funded through the Department of Education attended a national training center in drug education in the summer of 1970. Upon return they developed workshops in drug abuse education, stressing alternatives to drug abuse and involving communities in planning approaches to the problem. A resource book and many educational materials have been developed to aid in these workshops, which include health personnel, teachers, students, law enforcement and community people. Three day workshops have been and will be held in Anchorage, Fairbanks, Kenai, Nome and Juneau involving from 60-110 people in each. Contact: Mary Beth Hooten, Health Education Consultant to Drug Abuse Education, Department of Education, Pouch F, Juneau 99801.

California—The State Office of Narcotics and Drug Abuse Coordination is compiling information on: existing prevention, treatment and rehabilitation programs; arrest statistics, location, sociological factors; existing drug abuse movies, audiovisual aids, books, pamphlets; and current drug research.

The Department of Education has completed *A Study of More Effective Education Relative to Narcotics, Other Harmful Drugs and Hallucinogenic Substances* and *A Framework for Health Instruction in California Public Schools, K-12*. This document is designed to serve as a foundation for local curriculum development and contains a section on "Drug Use and Misuse." Several statements, such as "Basic Considerations Relating to Drug Abuse Education," have been developed by the Department and distributed to schools and community groups. The Office of Narcotic and Drug Abuse Coordination was established by the Governor in February 1970. The California Inter-Agency Council on Drug Abuse continues to work through its six Task Forces—Education, Youth, Treatment, Research, Administration of Justice, Legislation and Government. The Task Force on Education has passed resolutions on : (1) Professional Preparation of

Certificated School Personnel, (2) Community Drug Abuse Education Programs, (3) Educational Policy Determination, (4) In-Service Training of Personnel in Drug Education, (5) Desired Characteristics of School Personnel Involved with Drug Education Responsibilities, (6) The Primary Responsibility of Schools Relative to Drug Education, (7) Drug Abuse Education: Guidelines for Rental, Purchase and Use of Instructional Materials and Audio-Visual Media. The resolutions are available to any groups wishing to utilize them. Contact: Patricia Hill, Consultant in Health Education, Bureau of Health Education, Physical Education, Athletics, and Recreation, State Department of Education, 721 Capitol Mall, Sacramento 95814.

Colorado—The 1970 General Assembly passed two Acts funding, in the Departments of Education and Health, a community education program for Colorado emphasizing the problems of alcohol and drug abuse. This legislation envisions a comprehensive program reaching "members of the various health professions including mental health workers, nurses, and other health aides, social workers, students, institutions of higher education, parents, and the community at large, as well as teachers and children in the public schools." An interdepartmental task force of the Colorado Inter-departmental Committee on Alcohol and Drug Abuse has been set up to formulate, implement and evaluate the program. The Committee recommends that each school district in Colorado adopt into its K-12 curriculum meaningful health units which include education on alcohol and other drugs. It is suggested that these units should be integrated into existing curriculum in order to avoid undue focusing of attention on specific areas such as illicit drugs. Also, school districts are encouraged to shift their emphasis from traditional methods of teaching about drugs, primarily the teaching of cognitive data on substances, and concentrate instead on people and their needs.

The Legislative Council Interim Committee on Mental Health and Mental Retardation appointed a Task Force on Drugs and Alcohol to assist the Committee in its study of alcoholism and drug abuse and to suggest recommendations about the state's role in these programs. Among the subjects studied are: the existing and proposed education programs; the need for treatment facilities; the incidence of drug abuse; existing laws on narcotics, marijuana, dangerous drugs; and the kind of approach needed at the state level. The Legislative Council Interim Committee on Mental Health and Mental Retardation has completed a two year study, part of which was devoted to drugs and alcohol. The Committee made its recommendations in a final report to the 1971 General Assembly. Contact: Janice R. Schneider, Project Director, State Department of Education, State Office Building, Denver 80203.

Connecticut—The Department of Education developed, printed and distributed 5,000 copies of a set of guidelines covering the legal, health, and community aspects that must be considered in formulating a school policy. A broad spectrum curriculum guide was prepared. A guide prepared by the Stamford (Conn.) public schools is also in wide use. There is considerable cooperation among the Departments of Education, Health, Mental Health and Higher Education in preparation of educational programs for public schools and teacher pre-service preparation. Seven persons including a high school student attended the U.S.O.E. workshop in Chicago, and this team developed a state plan which was funded at full allocation, $49,000. The elements included establishing the position of Drug Education Coordinator and setting up the mechanism for grants to local schools to facilitate teacher in-service preparation. Continual efforts to keep advised of the status of drug education at all school levels have been marked by the following items: (a) a survey in May, 1970 by the Department of all public school systems' activities in drug, alcohol and nicotine/smoking education (which showed 85.6% of the responding schools had educational programs in grades 6-12), and (b) participation in the design of a survey by the Department of Mental Health relative to high school principals' evaluation of ex-addict presentations and roles in school programs. In addition, the Department will be utilizing information gathered by the Commission for Higher Education on both pre-service and in-service teacher preparation activities in the colleges and universities. Contact: Donald J. Anneser, Drug Education Coordinator, Connecticut Department of Education, Box 2219, Hartford 06115.

Delaware—Through a grant from the United States Office of Education, a statewide drug education leadership and training session has been held. The session served as the frame of reference for local school district training sessions to be conducted during the course of the school year. School personnel and community representatives participate in the training sessions. Contact: Dr. Randall L. Broyles, Director, Secondary Education, State Department of Public Instruction, P.O. Box 697, Dover 19901.

District of Columbia—The Narcotics Treatment Administration conducted a study with regard to (a) the extent to which drug addiction exists in the city of Washington, (b) the effectiveness of the city's own narcotics treatment programs and the effectiveness of other privately run treatment programs under contract to the city, (c) issues in the area of drug addiction, e.g., the relationship of addiction to criminal activity, characteristics of the addict population, events in the treatment process, etc. and (d) the impact of the city's educational programs. Contact: Vincent Reed, Public Safety Director, Presidential Building, Room 1205, 415 12th Street, N.W., Washington, D.C. 20004.

Florida—The Governor's Task Force on Narcotics, Dangerous Drugs and Alcohol Abuse reported in May 1970 on the scope of drug abuse in Florida. The State Board of Education has announced emergency regulations including instruction for all children in grades kindergarten through 12 in drug abuse education before the end of the 1970-71 school year. Beginning with the 1970-71 school year, the division of elementary and secondary education conducted a series of regional clinics on drug abuse for professionals, para-professionals and personnel of non-school related agencies. Beginning with the school year 1971-72: drug abuse education was planned as a regular and required unit of instruction in junior high school and at the senior high school levels. School districts were asked to schedule, as a component of the staff development plan, training sessions designed to provide teachers with current information and knowledge of the harmful effects of drugs, narcotics, alcohol and tobacco and other immediate health related concerns. All teacher preparation institutions and junior colleges require drug, narcotic, alcohol and tobacco education as a major component of health education courses. Contact: Louis Morelli, State Department of Education, 377 Knott Building, Tallahassee 32304.

Georgia—The Department of Education and the Georgia Kiwanis Clubs co-sponsored a youth conference on drug use and abuse in 1969 and again in November 1970. The 1969 conference was video taped by the Educational Television Division and tapes have been used extensively. The Division of Curriculum Development formulated and distributed a teacher guide in drug abuse education, *Viewpoint*, to all schools in the state and has developed and distributed over 6,000 comprehensive resource kits to schools, teachers, students, law enforcement offices and other interested persons. In addition, the staff met with all curriculum directors and other personnel at the local system level having responsibility for instructional programs and discussed new developments, guide formulation, curriculum content and use of audio-visual aids in instruction. Educational television assisted in the Department's efforts with special programs, such as a series for students, and teacher in-service and out-of-school populations. A U.S. Office of Education funded program provided training in drug abuse education for three hundred seventy persons designated by local school districts. Contact: Jack B. Short, Coordinator, Health, Physical Education and Recreation—Driver and Safety Education, Georgia Department of Education, State Office Building, Atlanta 30334.

Hawaii—During the 1970 legislative session a number of laws were enacted appropriating money for the study of the drug problem. Act 156 appropriated a sum of $15,000 for a study to develop a state program for the rehabilitation of drug addicts. Act 127 appropriated money to the Office of the Governor in order to develop educational and rehabilitation projects with private non-profit organizations, as well as to help county agencies in enforcing controls. The Department of Education, along with the Departments of Social Services, Health, and Budget and Finance, planned a program to combat drug abuse, based on the San Diego drug education program. Contact: Jeanne

Paty, Program Specialist, Health Education, Department of Education, P.O. Box 2360, Honolulu 96804.

Idaho—Idaho's drug abuse education approach is community-oriented. A youth-adult conference to determine the needs of students was scheduled in December, 1970. The conference led to the scheduling of six regional one week workshops to train 5-6 man teams from local communities including two students. At the local level these teams were to stimulate community involvement in programs emphasizing drug abuse among a wider range of community values. The Idaho program was funded by a $40,000 EPDA grant and $20,500 from the State Law Enforcement Planning Agency. Contact: Harold R. Goff, Executive Director, Idaho Consortium, State Department of Education, Boise 83707.

Illinois—The Department of Education offered 18 one-day seminars throughout the state. Illinois has an Inter-Agency Drug Abuse Education Development Committee which is composed of representatives from the Illinois Departments of Public Health, Mental Health, Bureau of Investigation and the Governor's Office of Human Resources. This group resolved cooperatively to develop a curriculum guide. Contact: Thomas M. Janeway, Director, Health Education, Division of Instruction, Office of Public Instruction, 316 South Second Street, Springfield 62706.

Iowa—The Iowa legislature considered the Uniform Drug Act in the 1971 session, and anticipated the need for increased appropriations for rehabilitation of drug abusers. The education program includes training of teachers and drug abuse education for K-12. Adult education at the community level is being encouraged. Contact: John Menefee, Department of Public Instruction, Grimes State Office Building, Des Moines 50319.

Kentucky—The federal government provided a grant of $53,000 for developing an education program, a coordinated approach by the Departments of Mental Health, which has primary responsibility, Public Safety and Education. Emphasis was placed on making responsible officials and parents aware of the magnitude of the problem. A task force was organized to conduct regional drive-in workshops to train various groups, i.e., teachers, lawyers, and young professionals under thirty years of age to assist in working with youngsters, elementary students—fifth and sixth graders—as well as high school students. In the public schools, unit courses in science or biology are the vehicle most used for drug education. The Department of Mental Health's Division of Regional Services was instrumental in placing alcohol education programs in colleges and universities for the 1970 spring term. Thirty institutions agreed to offer this course for credit in the 1970 fall term. Contact: Sidney Simandle, Director, Division of Teacher Education and Certification, State Department of Education, State Office Building, Frankfort 40601.

Kansas—A seven member state team participated in a National Training Institute and planned a one week statewide leadership training conference for 14 regional teams of ten members each. Regional team members would return to local areas and plan and conduct two day follow-up leadership conferences. Every school district and community were invited to send representatives. Participants in the regional leadership training programs would return to local communities and conduct a program for the teachers and community. Contact: Carl Haney, Health Consultant, State Department of Education, 120 E. 10th Street, Topeka 66612.

Louisiana—The State Department of Education in cooperation with local education agencies and numerous state agencies and organizations scheduled seven drug education information conferences. Each program was divided into five areas of concern: pharmacology, sociology, psychology, law enforcement, and teaching techniques. These conferences are designed to insure extensive involvement of a cross section of professional educators and interested citizens in the training of personnel for drug education in schools throughout the state. Funds for the development of this drug education program were secured through the Education Professions Development Act for a period of one year. The 1970 Legislature enacted two laws regarding refilling of depressant or stimulant drug prescriptions and equalizing penalties for possession and control of narcotic and hallucinogenic drugs. Contact: Harold Denning, Director of Planning and Evaluation, State Department of Education, Baton Rouge 70804.

Minnesota—Three demonstration projects were funded by a federal grant to develop and implement a comprehensive drug abuse education program which included in-service education programs for teachers, school administrators, counselors, nurses, and social workers. All education majors attending teacher education institutes are required to complete a course in drug abuse education before they can be certificated to teach in Minnesota.

In addition to the three programs under the direction of the State Department of Education, the Governor's Drug Abuse Commission also initiated a community education effort. Four regional coordinators, hired through federal LEAA (Law Enforcement Assistance Administration) funds, were made available to assist local communities in forming comprehensive cooperative programs under the coordination of a Citizen Action or Youth Environment Council. As of December, 1970, 100 councils had formed or begun operation.

The Commission on Drug Abuse operates as a statewide coordinating agency to maximize the effectiveness of the seven State Departments and number of major agencies working in areas related to drug abuse. The Commission decided to open a statewide clearinghouse in late December with a single phone number publicized statewide, that could be called toll free from anywhere in the state.

Governor LeVander's Drug Abuse Commission and its advisory committees recommended to the Minnesota Legislature establishment of a statutory state coordinating body; changes in the existing penalty structure; increased counseling and treatment facilities for drug abusers; and additional educational programs in the schools and the general community.

Missouri—The Missouri Department of Education initiated a statewide drug education training program under the National Drug Education Training Program. Regional training programs for teachers and community representatives were established to offer all local school districts in the state the possibility of having at least one person trained in the area of drug education. Consultant help was also made available to local school districts to plan local programs in drug education. The Governor appointed a state advisory committee on drug abuse to make recommendations concerning legislation and possible programs. The Division of Mental Health, the Missouri Highway Patrol, the Law Enforcement Agency, St. Louis College of Pharmacy, local drug councils, and other agencies and organizations throughout the State have conducted workshops, held meetings and sponsored various other activities relating to drug abuse. Contact: Jack E. Roy, Director, Education Professions Development Act, State Department of Education, Jefferson City 65101.

New Jersey—Senate Bill No. 748, an act authorizing the establishment of workshop programs of instruction on the problems of drug abuse by young people, was funded in 1968 at $50,000 for programs in narcotic and drug abuse education for elementary and secondary teachers in the public schools of New Jersey. It was re-funded for the 1969-70 school year and conferences were conducted. In 1970, as the result of a special message to the legislature by Governor William Cahill, Assembly Bill 1056 was passed and signed into law, authorizing the Commissioner of Education to establish summer workshops to train selected teachers to teach drug programs to secondary school teachers and to establish drug education training programs for teachers in school districts containing secondary school grades. Also each school district having secondary school grades would incorporate into its health education curriculum a drug education unit during a minimum of 10 clock hours per school year. The Act also provides for operational grants directly to the local school districts according to a formula based upon school district population in grades 7-12. The Commissioner was also directed to develop an evaluation procedure of the effectiveness of the drug education program and report to the State Board of Education. A New Jersey proposal to continue training of teacher trainers in grades 7-12 was approved for a $91,000 EPDA grant. Subsequent legislation introduced in New Jersey emphasizes education and rehabilitation. Contact: William Burcat, Division of Curriculum Instruction, State

Department of Education, 225 West State Street, Trenton 08625.

New York—The Education Department is directing a six-part drug education program, spearheaded by immediate team and teacher training, emphasizing a "peer group" approach which follows the reasoning that students are far more concerned with what their peers think about drugs than what adults think or say. The program includes: school-community team training; in-service training of present teachers; expansion of curricular offerings; intensive health teacher-training program; grants for local drug education projects and a college volunteer program. One hundred fifty teachers attended Adelphi University in the summer and fall of 1970. These graduates were expected to return to their districts where they would instruct about 6,000 elementary and secondary teachers in drug education. To prepare secondary health education teachers who would have the major responsibilities for drug education, six courses of six-weeks duration were held for 300 health educators. Considering drug education to be more than a study of pharmacology, the Department decided to make mental health education a prerequisite to drug studies. Drugs and their implications for the area of safety are also stressed. The Department programs stress involvement of the community as a whole in the search for solutions to the drug problem.

Four 5-day school-community summer workshops and one fall workshop were held to assist local school districts in developing or improving their district plan. A college volunteer program on ten campuses involving approximately 20 students at each was started in 1970. After attending from four to five concentrated weekend organizational development sessions, volunteers would then begin work with campus, elementary and secondary school-age persons providing up-to-date accurate information about drugs, counseling prospective users to change their behavior, and helping public and non-public school students to organize their own councils.

Education's Role in the Prevention of Drug Abuse was distributed to all school district administrators in the fall of 1970. The guidelines contain information on the "Nature of the Problem," "School District Policies and Procedures," "Pro-gram Development," "Health Education," and "Legal Considerations." Curriculum materials on drug education start at the fourth grade level and continue on to the high school levels. Grades four through six study early man's use of drugs, modern drugs and their contributions, and the use and misuse of drugs. Grades seven through nine learn the nature of drugs and how they work, the safeguarding of drugs, and the facts about habit forming and addicting drugs. Students in grades 10 through 12 discuss drug dependence, use and abuse of narcotic drugs, use and abuse of stimulants, the hallucinogenic drugs, drug traffic, legislation, and rehabilitation of the addict. Built into the program is a feed-back system enabling the Education Department to determine results and reactions periodically.

To implement this comprehensive educational program against drug abuse, approximately $1,100,-000 in state funds and $200,000 in federal funds were made available to the Education Department. Intensive teacher training, team training, school-community workshops, curriculum preparation and local pilot projects used about $800,000. The remaining $300,000 was earmarked for the college volunteer program. Federal funds were used for the in-service courses at Adelphi University. A $65 million state legislative appropriation made available in 1970 must be matched on a fifty-fifty basis by local contributions. Contact: John Sinacore, Chief, Bureau of Health Education, State Department of Education, Albany 12224.

North Carolina—The public school system demonstrated a great deal of concern about drug abuse problems, and teachers trained during the summer of 1970 continued planning and implementing in-service training classes in addition to various other types of school drug education programs. A legislative Drug Abuse Commission completed an interim report on drug abuse statewide. The subcommittee on education tentatively recommended: an education program to reach into the elementary grades; development of a policy for dealing with drug users and pushers in the public schools, mandatory inclusion of a course in drugs and drug abuse in all state colleges; requesting teachers to take an accredited course on drugs and drug abuse; and a concerted effort to educate the public. Contact:

Robert Frye, Drug Education Coordinator, State Department of Public Instruction, Raleigh 27602.

Ohio—The 1970 General Assembly enacted H.B. 874, which requires the Department of Mental Hygiene and Correction to establish special facilities for the treatment and rehabilitation of drug dependent persons. The law requires the public school curriculum to include instruction on the harmful effects and legal restrictions against the use of drugs of abuse, alcohol, and tobacco; defines drugs of abuse, drug dependent persons and persons in danger of becoming a drug dependent person; provides a procedure whereby a trial court may place drug dependent offenders on probation on condition that they undergo treatment for their drug dependence; revises the definition of "mentally ill individual" to extend application of these laws relating to treatment and hospitalization of the mentally ill to drug dependent persons; provides that minors 16 and over may apply on their own behalf for admission to a mental hospital for treatment of drug dependence or danger of drug dependence; legalizes the methadone treatment for incurable narcotics addicts, when administered under controlled conditions; requires the Department of Mental Hygiene and Correction to establish special facilities for the treatment and rehabilitation of drug dependent persons; redefines cannabis as an hallucinogen, thus making first offense possession of marijuana a misdemeanor; enacts a prohibition against glue-sniffing; increases penalties for certain offenses involving dangerous drugs (paregoric, codeine cough syrups, and others); permits the common pleas court to grant immunity to witnesses whose testimony is necessary to a drug investigation or prosecution; requires the court, in determining whether to place a drug offender on probation, to consider whether or not the offender has cooperated with law enforcement authorities investigating drug traffic; revises, without substantive change, the narcotics possession statute; and prohibits driving while under the influence of a drug of abuse. Contact: Woodrow W. Zinser, Director, Division of Drug Education, State Department of Education, 781 Northwest Blvd., Columbus 43212.

Oklahoma—A Narcotics and Drug Education Section was formed in the Department of Education.

Workshops, emphasizing communication between teachers and students, are intended to train personnel who can return to their local schools to teach and counsel others in this subject. Workshop instructors were trained at the National Drug Education Seminar in San Antonio, Texas. The Education and Health Departments conducted two college credit workshops for teachers. Regional workshops were scheduled during fall 1970. Future plans include the development of a curriculum guide for grades K-12. The focus of the Oklahoma Drug Education Program is on student-teacher communication. A major effort is being made to break down some of the cultural barriers between the two groups. Contact: Nevin Starkey, State Department of Education, State Capitol Station, Oklahoma City 73105.

Oregon—The Oregon Board of Education and the alcohol and drug section of the Mental Health Division jointly were responsible for a $20,305 project to provide materials and three teacher resource handbooks for use in the schools. *Toward Responsible Drug Education*, K-4, 5-9, and 10-14 were field tested by some 2,800 classroom teachers and administrators and disseminated to all schools. A federal, state and local community project was organized to provide drug education training for Oregon teachers. This project provided for Oregon teachers a forty-hour clinic-type in-service training program. Each teacher trained would be able, in turn, to train other teachers. The basis of the training would concentrate on the implementation of the teacher resource handbooks. The next project would attempt to tie previous efforts into a four-pronged prevention program; identifying specific responsibilities regarding drug abuse and assigning these responsibilities where they rightfully belong—to the parent, the school, the student, and the total community. Contact: James D. Goddard, Education Specialist, Health and Physical Education, State Board of Education, 942 Lancaster Drive, N.E., Salem 97302.

Pennsylvania—Through a U.S.O.E. grant, the Department of Education launched a statewide program on drug abuse education. Six colleges and universities were designated as training centers to assist the department in training leadership teams from school districts, colleges and universities. (The plan includes evaluation of workshops.) Contact: Robert G. Zeigler, Coordinator, Division of Health, Physical and Conservation Education, Department of Education, Box 911, Harrisburg 17126.

Puerto Rico—In March, 1970, six orientation centers for the prevention of drug addiction were organized in five of the six educational regions under the auspices of the Department of Education, the Narcotics Commission and the Crime Control Commission. They would serve an average of 12 towns in each region and would develop a program of primary and secondary prevention. In the primary prevention phase the efforts of this personnel would be directed to the training, organizing and strengthening of the local school team composed of the principal, social worker, guidance counselor and health educator, so that they could develop an action plan in accordance with the specific problems of their school and community. This phase included intensive training of teachers in the following areas: Knowledge of the characteristics of the developmental phases of their students; capacity to promote positive classroom experiences which will strengthen the students' personality; nature of the drug problem and how to deal with it; ability to detect factors in the school and in the family which may hinder the children's development; ability to identify early signs of emotional maladjustment in the students and how to cope with them; improvement of relations among school personnel. In this phase attention was also given to improving the relationships and communication between parents and children. Each orientation center began its program in three schools, elementary, junior high and senior high school level. As soon as the personnel of these schools were adequately trained, the team would move to another set of three schools. About 12,000 students, 350 teachers and other school personnel, and about 8,000 parents were involved in the primary.

The secondary prevention phase gave attention to the students who were referred by the teachers through the school social worker and called for a complete evaluation by the team. The staff would design and implement a plan of treatment for each student. Those students requiring additional or prolonged help would be referred to other governmental or private agencies. Contact: Mrs. Virginia Belaval, Health Program, Department of Education, San Juan 00919.

South Carolina—The State Department of Education completed a series of five regional workshops designed for the purpose of developing an awareness relative to drug use and abuse with a cadre of key teachers and students who would design and conduct similar workshops at the local level. The local workshops would involve plans for other teachers, students, and community leaders. Approximately 250 teachers and students were invited to attend the regional workshops, the nature of which was to involve presentations, discussions, and feedback relative to the causative agents for drug abuse, the pharmacological aspects, the physiological influences on the human system, the legal aspects, sociological implications, and treatments and potential treatment needs. Contact: Albert H. Dorsey, Chief, Curriculum Development Section, State Department of Education, Columbia 29201.

South Dakota—A survey of the status of drug abuse education was completed in September 1970 by the State Legislative Research Council. Among the recommendations were that the main focus of the effort should be at the local level, with state advice and support; that a state coordinating agency be named; that a state clearinghouse on drug information and a statewide directory of drug abuse resources be established. South Dakota's major drug education effort centers about the planning and implementation of a comprehensive lower grades to senior high school drug education curriculum. The Department of Public Instruction planned a K-12 program. Teacher training was handled by the South Dakota Drug Education Project through seven three-day workshops. These workshops also trained students and community leaders. It has been suggested that the state hire one or two fulltime drug education specialists to present elementary and secondary school teacher workshops on drug education around the state. There is considerable interest in use of the Educational Television Board and Instructional Television Council in programs on drug education. Contact: Richard Nankivel, Director, Health and Physical Education, State Capitol Building, Pierre 57501.

Texas—Six committees and the Crime and Narcotics Advisory Commission were created by the 61st Legislature (1969). The six committees studied drug abuse among and rehabilitation programs for youth, the problems of heroin addiction, the availability and use of narcotics and dangerous drugs, the control of availability of marijuana, crime and narcotics, and narcotics generally.

The Texas Education Agency adopted a statement of philosophy for drug education programs. The points include the following: Such a program must have total community planning and implementation. The overall objective is the minimization of the incidence of crime and drug misuse among the youth. The instructional program must stress attitude information and an effective behavior change. A "crash program" is questionable. The curriculum should not be further fragmented to incorporate drug and crime information; such information should be included in existing programs and be multidisciplinary in its approach. Extra-curricula activities are equally as important as the regular curricula. Drug Education should present the truth and deal with facts. It should not preach, moralize or use scare tactics. The focus must be on people. Facts about people are equally as important as those about crime and drugs, if not more so. The selection of the teacher is a key factor for the success of any program for crime and drug misuse. The teacher must be well grounded in the physiological, psychological and sociological disciplines. Administrators must be involved and have a clear understanding of the program content and techniques necessary to provide leadership and support of staff in program development. The program must focus on the positive and constructive use of drugs in our society. Contact: Dr. Louise Dooley, Project Director, Texas Education Agency, Austin 78711.

Utah—Utah's training program includes: Participation by a five person team in the National Drug Training Center at San Francisco State College, summer 1970; a one week "live in" seminar on drugs and drug abuse, communication, and alternatives to drugs for eight regional teams, November 1970; approximately twenty-two local district and/or regional teacher in-service seminars involving all of Utah's forty school districts, 1970-71

school year. Health education, biological science, social studies, and language arts teachers coupled with school counselors will be sought out as the primary target group of secondary teachers to reach. Three specific results are anticipated. Improved communication between students and school leaders. Students and school and community leaders will be encouraged to explore meaningful alternatives to drug use at the local school and community level, including improved school curriculums and recreational opportunities, and student involvement. Students will be involved at all levels of planning. Contact: Robert L. Leake, Specialist, Health, Physical Education and Recreation, Office of the Superintendent of Public Instruction, 1400 University Club Building, Salt Lake City 84111.

Vermont—The Drug Rehabilitation Commission compiled statistics on both the extent of drug abuse in Vermont and on the casualties resulting from such use. Contact: Dr. Edward Scully, Department of Education, State Office Building, Montpelier 05602.

Virgin Islands—During July and August, 1970, the Virgin Islands sent two teams of educators, students, public health personnel, and community representatives to Drug Education Workshops. In mid-October a coordinator for drug education was appointed by the Department of Education. Working with the two teams trained during the summer workshops, the coordinator was responsible for developing training workshops for each of the three islands. Emphasis was placed on involving youth in both the design and participation of the workshops. Initially the workshops involved students, teachers and administrators of both public and non-public schools and provided information concerning drugs and drug programs, taught participants techniques and methods for presenting drug information, and attempted to stimulate and develop new approaches to viewing, understanding and working with the drug abuse situation in the Virgin Islands. The initial workshop was planned for December, 1970. It was expected that participants of that workshop (who would be representing the various schools on the island of St. Thomas) would then organize training workshops within their own school facilities and further serve as school "task force" members in developing curriculum for all grade levels of students. Contact: Don Bachaus, Coordinator for Drug Education, Box 630, Charlotte Amalie, St. Thomas 00801.

Washington—The Legislative Council studied the extent of drug abuse in Washington as well as the rehabilitation and treatment programs available. The legislation proposed in 1971 dealt with control mechanisms for community sponsored drug abuse treatment facilities, as well as the granting of immunity to those undertaking treatment in these as well as state-operated facilities. Contact: Carl J. Nickerson, Drug Education Consultant, State Office of Public Instruction, Olympia 98501.

West Virginia—At the request of the Joint Committee on Government and Finance, the Legislative Services Agency, with the assistance of the Department of Public Safety and Department of Mental Health, gathered information for a status report for the 1971 legislative session. Recommendations anticipated the enactment of legislation to reduce penalties for users, particularly marijuana and increase penalties for pushers. It also anticipated an appropriation to Department of Public Safety for increase in specialization of personnel and for enforcement. Contact: Jerry Brewster, State Department of Education, Capitol Building, Charleston 25305.

Wisconsin—The Department of Public Instruction implemented a new law on Critical Health Problems Education adopted in February 1970. A consultant was added to the staff and an EPDA project on drug education carried out through state and regional training teams. The Secretary of the Department of Health and Social Services appointed a drug dependence program coordinator to handle liaison with other departments and agencies concerning programs and information on the treatment and rehabilitation of drug dependent persons and persons who abuse drugs. Various agencies are involved in collecting specific statistics on various aspects of drug abuse. The Department of Justice collects arrest statistics; the division of family services collects information on juvenile arrests and dispositions; the division of health has information on drug poison records from hospitals; the division of mental hygiene has information on patients at mental hospitals and related facilities. Under the terms of a 1969 act, the drug abuse control commission is directed to deliver a biennial report in January of each odd numbered year to the governor and the legislature reviewing state activities in the area of drug abuse prevention and control and making recommendations for further legislation. Contact: Luida Sanders, Department of Education, 126 Langdon Street, Madison 53702.

Special Supplement, "Drug Education in the States," from *Compact*, December, 1970, published by The Education Commission of the States. Excerpts slightly edited.

INDEX